THE PLEDGE OF A LIFETIME

Her Hope for **Connection.**

His Guide through **Conflict.**

MARK T. OELZE, MA

WESTBOW PRESS
A DIVISION OF THOMAS NELSON
& ZONDERVAN

Copyright © 2014 Mark T. Oelze, MA.
Edited by Christy Wold.
Cover layout by Steven Wold.

All rights reserved. No part of this book may be used or reproduced by any means, graphic, electronic, or mechanical, including photocopying, recording, taping or by any information storage retrieval system without the written permission of the publisher except in the case of brief quotations embodied in critical articles and reviews.

Scriptures taken from the Holy Bible, New International Version®, NIV®. Copyright © 1973, 1978, 1984, 2011 by Biblica, Inc.™ Used by permission of Zondervan. All rights reserved worldwide. www.zondervan.com The "NIV" and "New International Version" are trademarks registered in the United States Patent and Trademark Office by Biblica, Inc.™ All rights reserved.

Scripture quotations are from The Holy Bible, English Standard Version® (ESV®), copyright © 2001 by Crossway, a publishing ministry of Good News Publishers. Used by permission. All rights reserved.

Bible translations used: (all are duly noted in the body of the manuscript itself)
New International Version
English Standard Version
The Voice

WestBow Press books may be ordered through booksellers or by contacting:

WestBow Press
A Division of Thomas Nelson & Zondervan
1663 Liberty Drive
Bloomington, IN 47403
www.westbowpress.com
1 (866) 928-1240

Because of the dynamic nature of the Internet, any web addresses or links contained in this book may have changed since publication and may no longer be valid. The views expressed in this work are solely those of the author and do not necessarily reflect the views of the publisher, and the publisher hereby disclaims any responsibility for them.

Any people depicted in stock imagery provided by Thinkstock are models, and such images are being used for illustrative purposes only.
Certain stock imagery © Thinkstock.

ISBN: 978-1-4908-2440-6 (sc)
ISBN: 978-1-4908-2443-7 (e)

Library of Congress Control Number: 2014901663

Printed in the United States of America.

WestBow Press rev. date: 12/19/2014

How *The PLEDGE of a Lifetime* Is Helping People to Love Well:

"Lovingly relating in the middle of conflict (and all the time) is perhaps the highest value of a Jesus-revealing life, and the least understood and practical. My friend Mark's book goes a long way to providing clear understanding and practical instruction of what it means to actually love. I've read none better on the subject."

~Larry Crabb, Psychologist, Author

"I have known Mark and Zerrin Oelze for years… If I were to synthesize one of their life messages it would be, 'they are both committed to processing all of life's challenges with the love and wisdom of God.'

In addition Mark is a gifted counselor, speaker and teacher… Perhaps his most important teaching is the PLEDGE message, particularly when used as a tool to resolve conflict and enhance the quality of a relationship."

~Ken Canfield PhD.
Founder, National Center for Fathering

"… a practical guide to help couples who struggle to 'fight fair' learn new ways of responding to conflict… Mark's PLEDGE strategy incorporates simple, specific steps that are time-tested.

Mark has been an effective counselor for decades now. He is one of my personal mentors that I would refer my own children and family members to if they needed therapy. This book can revolutionize your marriage if you take the time to read it and put the PLEDGE steps into practice."

~Tony Wheeler, Ph.D.,
President and Director of The Family Ministry Institute,
Faculty Chair for Dr. John Trent's StrongFamilies.com

"… an engaging story of a couple learning to use the PLEDGE process to claim victory over conflict. We learned that we could use his Appendices and questions in our everyday relationships with our many new neighbors where we now live in an independent living facility."

~George and Marjean Fooshee
in their 59th year of marriage,
Founding Board Member of Crown Financial Ministries

"I love how Mark teaches these concepts through a story that I could see myself a part of. I laughed. I cried. I lamented my own failings. And I left longing for deeper connection with my wife and kids."

~Phil Mershon, M.Div. M.A.B.C.

"The step-by-step process of PLEDGE will change how you listen to, hear, and respond to others… God has used this method of communication to bring healing to our marriage!"

~Kim and Kim Cole, Business Owners

"Mark Oelze, in his genuine, caring, and engaging manner, delivers a story with practical and life-giving principles that can only revolutionize the way couples communicate—through a heart of love."

~Jo Lynn Bright, LCMFT

"…I thought of married couples I know who need this helpful tool. I found myself evaluating my own communication skills. Everyone can benefit from learning how to successfully navigate the troubled waters of communication by simply working the PLEDGE."

~Rodger Thompson, Pastor

"Mark's humility, caring heart, and faithfulness through decades of proven ministry to couples is reflected in this practical, easy to read, thought-provoking guide that contributes to a healthy life and marriage transformation."

~Steven Miller, China Harvest

"Going through the PLEDGE process to address conflict takes you and your spouse into a deeper conversation, thus a deeper connection, drawing you towards each other."

~Cassandra, Teacher/Homemaker

"This could be my husband and me that he's writing about… and it has made a world of difference in the way we communicate not only with each other, but also with our grown sons. We are so thankful for the skills we have learned so that we now really do try to listen to each other's heart."

~Barbara Livengood, retired Teacher

"This engaging 'real life' story is filled with great nuggets of insight and timeless truths… The book is priceless for healing and growing all kinds of relationships. We found the principles discussed to be very practical in our own lives… We highly recommend this book be read and re-read as couples, and the principles to be applied in your marriages, in your business and with your children. It really works!"

~Dr. David and Karla Dennis

CONTENTS

Foreword xi
Preface xv
Introduction xxi

To Reach for Help
    1. Longing for Connection............................ 1
    2. A Change in Direction.............................19
    3. Dialing Down and Shifting Focus 25
    4. Discovering the Heart of the Other 33
    5. A Critical but Forgotten Step 47

Putting It into Practice
    6. Keeping Perspective..................................61
    7. The Journey to Hope................................69

Governed by Love
    8. Doing it Right...93
    9. The Power of Validating 101
    10. A Rare Opportunity for Respect 107
    11. Moving from Confrontation to
        Conversation... 115

Epilogue 123
Afterword 125

Appendices
- The Mechanics of PLEDGE 129
- Questions & Answers About Using the PLEDGE Process 135
- Discussion Questions 143

Acknowledgements 147
About the Author 153

FOREWORD

After years of marriage and family counseling, Mark began to defend a simple yet powerful truth: people most effectively resolve conflict when they become strong communicators. He has written *The PLEDGE of a Lifetime* to give training in communication, an act we engage in everyday but so often practice poorly. Most of us are not even aware that we are inadequate communicators. Nor do we understand the heavy toll this takes on our relationships. Mark is uniquely qualified to teach us how to improve in this area. In addition to having been mentored by some of the nation's premier Christian counselors and leaders, he has spent three decades listening to marital communication and its breakdowns. While *The PLEDGE of a Lifetime* specifically engages communication within marriage, Mark's principles and strategies have demonstrated themselves successful in relationships of all sorts, from husband and wife, parent and child, and even in larger communities.

The trust placed in Mark extends to church congregations. Pastors all over the city, and now across the country, are asking Mark to lead marriage conferences. The insight he shares with couples, much of which is included here, has resulted in incredible testimonies so frequent that they now seem commonplace. But this consistent encounter with supernatural stories should come as no surprise. Everyone familiar with Mark's teaching walks away with the same revelation: by re-learning communication, we can all experience divine love on a daily basis.

Mark's efforts have been just as successful in his own home. Mark often says that children imitate their parents' habits, making practices "caught, not taught." But Mark both modeled and taught. He explained healthy practices of mediation to his children, even as they crawled into their first conflicts. The instilled phrase, "Daddy, we have a problem," was the five-year-old version of the "Pause" moment that initiates his PLEDGE process. As children and problems grew alike, Mark remained faithful to the process. The reward is a tight-knit family resulting in a warm home environment. Each of his children can engage him with tough conversations and still feel safe and loved.

Parenting PLEDGE is a challenge, especially to the ego. Mark's process holds humility as a prerequisite, since pride and defensiveness can rarely stand the two-way conversation of dialogue. While every father figure knows how to give a stern lecture, only a daring few will listen to, much less entertain, a son's perspective. The wise father recognizes that the act of listening is an act of valuing. When the son is given the chance to truly be heard, he feels drenched in the waves of his father's love and affirmation. These waves serve as baptism in the river of reciprocity. Standing once more on his feet, the son is finally ready—actually hoping—to hear his father's voice.

The PLEDGE of a Lifetime shares with its readers key principles of healthy communication that are critical to the process of conflict resolution. The text can be considered both menu and guide to a dinner table of conflict. Our culture seems to have just as many neuroses regarding food as we have phobias of conflict, making the metaphor particularly appropriate. Some of us are conflict-anorexics, obsessively avoiding arguments and even the smallest confrontations. Others of us tend to conflict-binge, compulsively lashing out with no limits, even as we are ashamed of our own interactions.

Certain interventions may be necessary for us to re-establish a healthy relationship with the conflict that life dishes up: these will no doubt include self-forgiveness and healing from the bad experiences of our past. At some point, however, we must turn to the challenges of the present. This text provides such a guide, inviting us to finally approach the conflict table with a confidence void of arrogance. Over time, we manage to stop rushing through arguments and choking down confrontations. We remember that the PLEDGE process itself occurs in courses (as some may want to read this book). Empowered by healthy communication practices, we begin to once again find the joy in dining. We recognize that the hot dish provides nourishment to our souls. Here we become stronger versions of ourselves and are graced with the companionship of those we hold most dear.

May my father's words encourage you to partake of this meal, that you may taste life in abundance.

Micah Oelze

PREFACE

For nearly 30 years, I have listened to the stories and struggles of husbands and wives. As a marriage and family counselor, it is a humbling opportunity each time I am invited into the private world of a couple. In recent years, I have observed two dynamics taking place in marriages with increased frequency:

1. Regardless of the issue, couples do not know how to talk through their conflicts in a healthy, love-filled manner.
2. Women in particular are giving up on their marriages in greater numbers than in years past. They are crying out for connection. However, by the time husbands awaken to the seriousness of the problem, the wives are finished, ready to walk away.

First Dynamic: Couples Lack Knowledge of How to Process Conflict

We all have moments of sudden clarity. Such a moment happened to me a few years ago. I was watching couple after couple in my office argue about their differences. The subject of the conflict didn't seem to matter; they just couldn't discuss the issue in a constructive manner. My light-bulb moment happened when I realized the "problem" isn't the problem.

Couples come to me complaining about sex, finances, affairs, communication, children, in-laws, alcohol, pornography, and more, but these aren't the real problem. Couples *think* these issues are the problem, but the real problem has to do with connection—they have none.

Think of the times when you're on your cellphone, talking on and on—when suddenly you realize you're talking to no one. The call was dropped. You were disconnected. Something went wrong with either the transmission of the call (ex. the battery went dead) or the reception (ex. out of range of a cell tower).

In marriage, there is a call for each partner to love the other well. But after the wedding ceremony, at some undetermined moment, there is a "disconnect." It can happen a thousand different ways and for as many reasons. Suddenly one party or the other realizes they are talking, but their spouse isn't listening. Something has gone wrong with either the transmission or reception; the *call to love* was dropped.

Instead of connecting, the pair becomes reactive and defensive, or they grow sullen and shut down. Understanding is rarely achieved. An appreciation of each other's perspective almost never occurs. They just don't get it.

When counseling these couples, over and over I want to jump into their arguments and challenge them: *Can't you see what she's trying to say, and why? Don't you realize how reactive you are and the effect it has on him?*

Second Dynamic: Wives Abandon Marriage

As I previously stated, women are giving up on their marriages in greater numbers than ever before. Close to 75% of my caseload is made up of couples who are at a crossroads: if they don't get help fast, the wife is ready to walk away from the relationship. The number one complaint from these women is that they can't connect with their husband.

A Note to Wives

To wives I say, don't give up.

We are all a work in progress. In the deepest core of your husband, I promise you, he wants to connect. He just doesn't know how, and he is afraid. I know—I'm a man. The method of conversing I teach in this book is a practical guide that, if used correctly, creates the connection you are longing for—especially in the throes of conflict.

If you read this book before your husband does, here is my advice.

- Read it through yourself at least twice.
- Begin to practice the principles on your own without telling your husband what you are doing.
- After a week or two, look for a time when you have your husband's attention. Tell him that you have a strong desire and need to connect with him on a deeper level.

- Show him the book. Tell him it is written by a man and that you believe it can really help. Humbly tell him that by reading the book yourself you have seen areas in your own life you need to change and are working on making that happen (if that is true, of course).
- Simply ask him if he, too, would read it. Then turn and get back to whatever you were doing just before you started talking to him. In other words, don't stand there for a response. It will make him feel pressured. By turning away, you give him the freedom to process what just happened and decide when and how he will respond. He needs this time and will be grateful for it, even if it's just a few moments.
- Keep in mind, some men aren't readers—if that is your husband, don't despise him for that. Instead, offer to read it with him out loud.

Your husband needs your encouragement more than you imagine. As every husband beholds his wife, he is attracted and drawn near. But as every man can also attest, the words, expressions, and actions of his wife can equally repel him when he experiences her contempt. That is what he fears. You feel vulnerable when you expose your heart to be loved—he might reject you. He feels vulnerable when his weaknesses are exposed—you might look on him with disdain.

No one on earth can have a greater impact upon him for better or for worse than you. May God give you the grace to become ever more beautiful in how you relate to your husband.

A Note to Husbands

To husbands I say, stay engaged.

Don't retreat from your marriage and family. They need you more than you know. No one on earth plays a more crucial role in the lives of your wife and children than you.

It is scary to engage relationally—I will admit that. Women tend to be better at it than men. I am convinced, however, that you can learn what it takes to stay connected, to communicate in a healthy manner even through conflict, and to love well. In this book, I will show you the way to do so. It will take work and focus. But if you truly want to love your kids and give them the best chance at life, if you are thankful for the woman in your life and want her to know beyond a doubt that she is loved—then you must face your fears and do the work. I challenge you to take this on as your mission. I use that word intentionally, because if there is one thing that stirs us as men, it is accomplishing a mission.

Interestingly enough, a surprising number of you men are now asking for help. Many of you have also had a light-bulb experience and want to know how you can save your marriage. I will show you a straightforward way to communicate with your wife, a step-by-step process of dialoguing that will be very helpful, particularly when it comes to conflict. This method is based upon solid principles of healthy communication. By using it as a guide in the exact order I have laid out, you will learn how to truly connect with your wife.

We all long to connect, but we often haven't quite known how. Men, now you can learn how. I have written this with you in mind. May God give you the courage to proceed.

My Hope for Your Marriage

This book is my response and endeavor to help all those who are caught in the web of unresolved conflict. I want you to know there is a way to get through the tension and grow closer together in the process. There is rich, meaningful conversation just waiting to be had with those whom you care about the most.

This is a book that has developed over years, maturing as I have witnessed thousands of heartbreaking battles between husbands and wives. My work with these couples, and our initial trial-and-error attempts to fix conflict, has resulted in a process that has borne much fruit. It is a step-by-step template that guides conversation through a method called PLEDGE. It enables couples to talk through and process conflict in a manner governed by love.

-Mark T. Oelze, MA-

INTRODUCTION

I was sitting across from a couple that had come in for marriage counseling. It was another case where a wife had lost hope in her marriage, having given up any effort to connect with her husband. He said he was totally shocked when he was handed divorce papers. He had no idea things were as bad as they were. The man seemed very genuine and willing to do whatever it took to keep their marriage intact and to grow to love each other once again. In his desperation, he looked at me and said with great passion, "I would die for my wife!"

I acknowledged the courage and love it would take for him to die for his wife. Then I looked at him squarely and asked, "But would you live for her?" It is one thing for someone to give their life for another—a truly noble act. It is an entirely different matter to live one's life for another.

The truth about everyone who has ever lived is that we are far more self-centered than we would like to believe. In all my years of counseling, I have never yet heard a parent speak of having to teach their children to be selfish—all children have that inclination from birth. The real task parents face is training their children how to share and be kind. That is, in fact, a lifelong challenge for each of us.

If we are honest, we must admit that even as adults we often don't know how to get past the tendency that resides in our hearts to think primarily about ourselves. We see the need, and we are aware at times that we want to love another. When it comes right down to it, though, getting past *self* is tough.

Perhaps nowhere is this more evident between a husband and wife than when they find themselves in the midst of a conflict. Emotions are riled, and feelings are hurt. Both want to be heard, but neither is really listening. And *self* is at the very center for both parties. Neither party even considers the idea of giving up their own desires and considering what is best for their spouse. As a result, the conversation goes from bad to worse. And every time, the disconnect between them gets stronger and stronger.

Writing About Conflict

In this book, I present a simple narrative that employs the PLEDGE process. PLEDGE is a communication tool to be used when working through all conflict, big or small. You will also discover how it goes beyond that to enhance all conversation. My hope is that by presenting this in story form, it will carry you along while it demonstrates PLEDGE in action.

The story that unfurls on the following pages is a glimpse into the struggling marriage between Jake and Lisa. They look for help from Mike, a marriage counselor. While the story itself is fictional, in a sense it is a true story as well. It is a composite of the countless stories I have heard from one couple after another as they have invited me into the midst of their conflict.

Come sit in and observe Jake and Lisa as they enter Mike's office. Peer into their hearts and minds. Listen to their struggles—the battles, the loneliness, the anger. But also watch their healing. Where did it start? How did it progress? What did it require on the part of each person? Finally, learn for yourself a process that claims victory over conflict while promoting ever-deepening love.

To Reach for Help

Chapter 1

LONGING FOR CONNECTION

"I can't believe you're telling me this!" yelled Jake. He knocked his chair over with a clatter and stomped toward the front door. "What did I do to deserve this?"

"Jake, come back!" cried Lisa, following him out to the driveway.

"I can't! I have to get away and think," growled Jake as he tried to contain his rage.

"I'm sorry! Really, I am! WAIT!" Lisa pleaded as Jake drove off, tires squealing, in his '94 Mustang convertible.

It seemed like an hour before her shock subsided and Lisa was able to go inside. She had no idea when or if he would return. How could all of this have happened? How could she have let *it happen? Maybe she shouldn't have even said anything—but she had already gone down that line of thinking and decided that wasn't a good option either. All she knew to do was hope and pray.*

As Lisa turned back towards the house, she saw all three kids standing in the doorway, tears streaming down their faces. Lisa did her best to hold it together and explain that she and Daddy had just had a bit of a disagreement. He needed a break and would be back shortly. She assured them they would talk it out and everything would be fine. She herded them into the kitchen, saying it was time for lunch.

All the while, Lisa fought back her fears of their future. Where would this lead?

****

Getting Started.

Jake and Lisa started out their marriage madly in love. They met in college, where they had several classes together. Jake first spotted Lisa from the back of the class. After several weeks of light talk and teasing, he asked her out to dinner. The evening went well. Both seemed mutually interested in the relationship, and it quickly evolved into an ongoing courtship.

Lisa reminisced that Jake planned one thing after another to make her feel wanted. It was like every step he took and every word he said was meant to win her over.

Jake reported that Lisa was quite charming. She would smile a lot and laugh at his jokes while elbowing him in the side. She often talked about how much fun she had being with him. Jake said it was like she always wanted to be by his side, and that was very affirming.

They dated six months before getting engaged and married eight months after that. Throughout their courtship, there was never any doubt they were meant for each other. They spent a great deal of their waking hours together, helped each other in various ways whenever possible, and truly enjoyed one another's presence. They had many shared values, along with a mutual desire to live life with a sense of adventure and mission. Both spoke often of how they wanted their lives to count for a greater good.

Three years into their marriage, they had their first child. They were excited for this season of their lives together. Two more children came shortly thereafter. Life was full but fun. Jake particularly enjoyed the two boys—Jackson, age twelve, and Cody, ten—and Lisa loved having Lea, their nine-year-old daughter, tagging alongside her. Jake and Lisa had just celebrated their 15th anniversary last month.

Everything sounds good so far, thought Mike, their marriage counselor. He had been listening to them both respond to his questions about how they had met and how their marriage together had progressed. "So, at what point were either of you aware that the relationship started to decline?"

There was a pause. Then Lisa said, "I don't know when it started exactly. All I know is that one day I remember thinking it didn't seem right between us. I longed for connection and it just wasn't happening. All our conversations seemed to end up in an argument or with us just ignoring each other. I tried over and over to get him to see there was a problem, but he never got it. Then one morning, I realized I was dreading seeing him at the end of the day."

"That caught your attention, huh?" said Mike, making it sound more like a statement than a question. He nodded with understanding as he looked at Lisa, sitting a few feet across from him on a soft leather couch.

"Yeah. I was actually really worried, but I didn't know what to do about it. I didn't want to say anything to Jake. That couldn't be good. I tried just brushing it aside, telling myself I was probably just in a bad mood. But then I noticed that my lack of excitement around him continued. I was afraid he might start to notice it, so I began to add things to my schedule—working out, going out with friends, working longer hours—using those things as an excuse for why we didn't have that much time together." Lisa's voice trailed off as she looked down at her hands twisted in her lap.

Mike waited for either of them to continue. Finally he asked, "What kind of impact did that have on you, Jake?"

Jake, who had been staring coldly at the opposite wall, crossed his arms and sighed. "Well, for a long time I didn't notice anything. I thought we were doing fine. After awhile, I started getting a bit frustrated that she was never around. Like, in the beginning, she wanted to spend every second with me, but then..." he shrugged. "I didn't know if I was just imagining things, or if she was mad at me, or what." He hesitated, his face darkening, "Most recently, I got to thinking maybe she was having an affair."

Lisa cleared her throat. "And that was another frightening thing happening to me. I did *not* have an affair—at least not physically," she stammered on the last few words. "I got emotionally involved with one of my co-workers. I didn't know what to do. I knew I still loved Jake—at least in my head—but here I was having feelings for another guy. It went on for a couple of months before I finally broke down and told Jake everything I just told you—a couple weeks ago. He—he got pretty upset. He yelled at me, and I started crying. Then he left the house, got in the car, and drove off." Lisa's voice sounded choked as she continued, "I thought he was leaving me. He came back after a couple hours, and we tried to talk it out but didn't get very far. That's when I suggested maybe we should see a counselor. I called my best friend the next day, because I remembered she and her husband had gone to counseling awhile back, and she gave me your name."

"Well, first, I want to say I really applaud you both for not giving up on your marriage and not giving in to the hurt and anger you're feeling. I also want to commend you both for seeking out someone to help. Unfortunately, in my line of work, most people come to me as sort of a last ditch effort on the way to an attorney. People come to me hoping I can perform some kind of miracle in their relationship that sets everything straight from the last ten years of hurt and pain. That just isn't possible. I wish it was, but it isn't. I tell people whenever I have the opportunity—'don't wait until the house is burned down to call for help. Please make that call instead when you simply have a fire in the kitchen.' So I'm glad you guys have come! It sounds like you have some real challenges ahead, but you want to make this work, is that correct?"

Lisa nodded and looked at Jake, who was sitting stiffly next to her on the couch. He tightened his lips and gave a slight nod.

Mike took a breath and asked, "Okay, from what you can see in your relationship as it stands now, where do you think you need the most help?"

After a moment, Lisa spoke first, looking hesitantly at her husband, "I'd say communication. It feels like Jake never listens to me or even tries to understand what I'm dealing with. He—"

Jake immediately went on the defensive, "I don't understand why she keeps saying that! I have heard every word she has ever said—and believe me, that's a lot of words 'cause she never stops talking!"

Lisa turned to Mike saying, "You see? He just doesn't get it!" and then turned back to glare at Jake. The hurt and anger between them suddenly sizzled.

Mike knew from experience that when emotions started to flare, he had to do something quickly before any further damage was done. He had been there before, all too often. Couples would come in to his office acting very respectful and professional, only to unashamedly end up in a verbal brawl within a very short time. At those moments, Mike felt more like a referee at a hockey game than a marriage counselor from whom couples were seeking help. So when the two began to snipe at one another, Mike interrupted their conversation and simply asked them to stop and be quiet a few moments. He wanted their emotions to dial down, and he needed some time to think.

Mike leaned back in his chair and closed his eyes for a moment. *How do couples get to this point? Why can't husbands and wives simply communicate their frustrations and concerns to each other in a better way? What goes wrong when they try?* He sighed and opened his eyes again.

"Is this typically what happens?" Mike asked finally. Not a brilliant question, but it was at least a start.

Lisa answered quietly, "Not all the time, but often enough."

"Are either of you okay with the way you handle conflict?"

"No," said Lisa dismally. Jake looked at the floor and shook his head.

"So, do you want to learn a different way?"

"Yes—I suppose that is ultimately what we need," she said as Jake gave a reluctant nod of consent.

Mike continued, "I can show you how. It will take a lot of work from both of you. You'll have to learn about yourselves and what it takes to communicate well. You'll also have to focus on a different way of interacting with each other. I can teach you a step-by-step method to process all conflict, big or small. I say process, because it will help you not only resolve conflict but learn from it. It will enhance all of your conversations, not only with each other but with everyone you know. I'm not exaggerating when I say that. It won't be easy—especially at first. But I promise it will pay huge dividends if you persevere and put into practice what I teach you, okay?"

"Yes, we can do that," Lisa said.

Jake remained silent.

Ingredients for a Good Conversation

"Okay—first let me ask you a few more questions," Mike said, glancing at Jake. "Both of you take a moment and tell me what you think are the necessary ingredients for a good conversation to take place—especially when you're working through frustrations with each other."

Lisa pursed her lips and said, "Well, I already told you a couple things I think are necessary. When I'm talking, I think he needs to listen and at least *try* to understand what I'm saying!"

"And *she* needs to say it with some kind of decency—without pointing her finger, and glaring at me, and telling me how I'm doing everything wrong!" added Jake.

In fear of another skirmish, Mike quickly jumped in to concur, "Good—you both are right on target. For good communication to take place, there *has* to be good listening on both sides. And not only listening, but understanding. It's critical that you do whatever it takes to truly understand each other. I don't have a statistic to back this up, but in my experience of working with couples for over 25 years, I believe one of the biggest reasons couples get into arguments is they're not taking the time to really understand what the other person is saying. Instead, they just react to what they hear on the surface and completely miss the core message."

Turning and addressing Jake, Mike said, "You mentioned the importance of *how* things are said to each other. That too is huge. Nobody likes it when someone is in their face, talking down to them, or yelling. Intuitively, we know there is a right way, a good way, to talk to each other, and we want to be spoken to in those ways." Still looking at Jake, Mike asked, "Do you remember how I said a few minutes ago that in order for this to work, you both will have to learn about yourselves?"

"Yeah—though I wasn't sure what all you meant by that," replied Jake.

"Well, here is a perfect example," Mike pressed on. "We all want to be spoken to in a way that we can hear what is really being said. For instance, a man will best be able to handle hearing something difficult when he's spoken to in a respectful manner. For women the same is also true, but in addition, most will better handle hearing something difficult when spoken to in a way that they feel safe, cared for, and loved."

Mike paused, giving them time to consider his words, and then continued, "Now here is the behavior we must recognize in and about ourselves: though we want to be spoken to a certain way, we rarely monitor how we speak to others! We are so quick to react to or judge how others speak to us. Yet rarely do we take time to consider what words come out of our mouths and even more importantly, *how* they come out. This is critical if you want to have good communication."

"That makes sense," Lisa commented. "I've never thought about it that way, but as a woman, I can relate to wanting to be talked to in a way that I feel secure."

"What about you, Jake?" Mike asked after a moment.

"Well," he answered, slowly at first, "I guess I've noticed when Lisa speaks to me in an affirming sort of way, it really makes me feel appreciated and even energized. Like just the other night when I came back from taking one of our vehicles to get the tires rotated, she said something about how she appreciated me taking care of the cars all the time. That really felt good—and made me feel a little less tired from the long day. Later that night, I asked her if there was anything I could help her with. Somehow there was a connection."

"Good observation, Jake. And good for you, too, Lisa," Mike said encouraged by their answers. "It's true. When a wife speaks in an affirming, respectful way to her husband, or when he speaks in a warm, loving way to his wife, it's life-giving. It's like oil in the engine, since you mentioned cars," Mike smiled, then went on, "It makes the relationship run smoothly, because the friction is taken out. And you're also right, Jake, about a connection taking place. When we're spoken to in a way that makes us feel loved and respected, it's as though something is energized inside of us that causes us to want to reciprocate that kindness.

"One other interesting point," Mike observed. "Notice how both of you just commented on how much you appreciate it when spoken to in a certain way. That's good. But neither of you picked up on the second point I made—that we rarely monitor how we speak to others."

"Actually, I did hear that," Jake said, shifting uncomfortably, "but I'm not sure what to do with that. When I'm mad, I probably don't think as much as I should about what I'm saying."

"At least you're honest, Jake," said Mike with a rueful grin. "Communicating well *does* take work, and it requires sacrifice on the part of each person. That is not our natural impulse in moments of conflict." Looking at Jake, Mike asked, "Did you ever play sports in school?"

"Sure," he said. "Mostly basketball."

"Were you any good?"

"Well, yeah, pretty good, I guess."

Lisa jumped into the flow of conversation, saying, "He was one of the best players on our college's team—and team captain his senior year! I remember my friends being *so* jealous when he started dating me." Lisa glanced at Jake with a reminiscent smile. Jake looked both surprised and pleased at her comment.

Mike chuckled, then asked Jake, "So did you just wake up one morning and suddenly realize you had incredible skills?"

Jake heaved a sigh. "No… and I know where you're going with this. I had to work hard—real hard. The game didn't come to me naturally. I only started playing 'cause when I was a kid, everyone said I should since my dad had been on the varsity team in high school and I was even taller than he was at my age. It wasn't easy at first. It took lots of time and practice. But I kept at it and got pretty good. I was a starter my last two years of high school and all four years in college. I really came to enjoy the game."

"You said you know where I'm going with this topic, Jake. I'm sure you probably do. Learning to communicate well with your wife won't come overnight. You *will* have to work at it—a great deal. It'll take a lot of time and sacrifice, especially at first. But if you do the work, you and Lisa will experience what it means to win together. Your kids will notice, too. And so will others. I want to challenge you to keep this in mind as we work together. I'm going to be your coach, and I'll do my best to teach you how to love well.

"Jake, you mentioned when we first talked today, that when you two were dating, you and Lisa both enjoyed a sense of adventure and mission. As men, we're stirred deeply by the sense of mission. We were made to rise up and meet the task at hand. When we do, there is a powerful sense of satisfaction."

Mike leaned forward and continued more fervently, "I know you love Lisa or you wouldn't be here, Jake, so stay with me on this. Learn everything you can. Do whatever it takes. Become the greatest lover you can be—that is one thing you will *never* regret."

After those last words, both Mike and Jake were quiet. Mike wasn't sure, but he thought he saw some red in Jake's eyes. He knew he felt the red in his own. "To say it another way," Mike cleared his throat and went on, "as men we were made to pursue a destiny, to impact the world around us. We must begin with our own families. I believe when we are called to this task in the right way, we will respond."

Mike waited, then got up and pulled over a whiteboard from behind his desk on the other side of his office. "Okay, getting back to having good communication and working through conflict..." he began jotting down some notes on the board. "We must be sure that good listening takes place; we must be sure we understand each other; and we must be careful what we say to another and how we say it. This takes work, and it takes sacrifice. Regularly, we must put aside what we want to say in order to hear what the other is sharing. So what else?"

They both thought for a moment. Lisa opened her mouth to speak then looked surprised when Jake spoke up again, "I'd say it's pretty important that we think before we speak. I guess it's related to that last point you just made, but I think it goes further, Mike."

"How so?"

"Well, it seems like whenever Lisa and I get into it, we just say the first thing that comes to mind. We don't think about what we're going to say or what the other person just said to us. We just—react."

Lisa grimaced and reluctantly added, "That's true. To continue with the sports theme, it's like we volley back and forth looking for those opportunities when we can spike it on the other person's side and score some points."

"Jake, I think that is a great insight—and a powerful analogy, Lisa. I actually hear two important principles in what you guys are saying. First, as you said, we so often tend to volley back and forth when arguing our points. We hardly give the person a chance before we strike back with our own thoughts. If we don't stop keeping score and break away from competing, we'll fail to realize that we're on the same team. We won't find or do what it takes in order for us to experience the win together.

"Secondly," Mike threw in, "we must stop and think about the why. Let me ask you this: what's the purpose of telling your spouse or friend you're frustrated with them? Are you simply doing it because you want to gripe? Is it because you're bored and just looking for something to do? Or is it maybe because you have been hurt or disappointed, and you want to hurt back?"

Jake and Lisa looked at each other uncomfortably and remained silent.

Mike put his marker down and continued, "Before you decide to talk with your spouse about a frustration, stop and ask yourself why you want to bring it up in the first place. If the purpose is one of the things I just mentioned, then I would strongly suggest you keep quiet. If on the other hand, you sense there is a good reason, then proceed—but with caution. For example, if you see how something said or done by your spouse is hurtful to your marriage or your children, it would be good to talk about it. Hopefully by doing so, you will bring greater health and love to your home.

"Notice, however, that I said to proceed *with caution*. Why? Because at any given moment while you're talking with your spouse about an issue, your ugly side might try to sneak in one more spike and score again. Unfortunately, that is part of our nature. We can really mean well and want to do the right thing, but when push comes to shove, we lose sight of the good and give way to evil.

"Here's one other helpful idea when considering whether or not to talk about a concern in your relationship. My wife and I have followed this general principle for most of our marriage. If at any time either one of us feels distant from the other, whether we understand the reason for the distance or not, we will talk about it. Keep in mind, we take care not to accuse each other. Rather, it's an occasion to think or talk together about what might be taking place between us—or what we might be lacking. The point is not for us to get things off our chest, though that may be part of what happens. The goal is to restore intimacy. It is to get back to love."

While Jake and Lisa were contemplating what he just said, Mike turned back to the whiteboard and started writing again. "So, two more points that we agree upon are: first, we have to find a way to stop the volleying back and forth and focus on winning *together*; and second, we need to answer the *why* and make sure the reason we bring up a concern to our spouse is to bring about goodness in our relationship and not evil."

Mike drew a breath then asked, "Okay, any more ideas of what brings about good communication?"

"Yeah," said Lisa. "I'm still thinking about the volleyball analogy. I don't know about Jake, but I think I know why I want to keep my words going over the net."

"Why is that?"

"Well, I feel like when I say something, he's so fast to throw my words right back at me, that I have to be strong and make sure I get my points across. It's like if I don't say what I'm thinking right away, I'm afraid I won't get the chance at all. So I won't give up or even stop talking until I know he hears me."

"And how often do you feel that happens? That he really hears you?"

She gave a hollow laugh and said, "I was just asking myself that. I don't feel like he *ever* hears me! As much as I keep flinging my words at him—and he does the same to me—it's like neither of us really gets our point across to the other. Something is not working right."

"Okay," Mike clarified, "So basically you're saying in order to connect relationally, you have to find a way for both of you to have the chance to talk while the other is really listening."

Jake smiled a little skeptically, "You make it sound so easy."

Chapter 1 Highlights

When talking with your spouse about a frustration, remember:

- Your husband will best be able to hear something difficult when you speak to him in a respectful manner.

- Your wife will best be able to hear something difficult when you speak to her in a way that she feels safe, cared for, and loved.

For successful communication and the ability to process conflict well:

- Good listening must take place.

- Both must seek to understand the other.

- Concern must be taken for *what* is said to another and *how* it is said.

- Volleying back and forth must cease. The focus must be on winning together.

- Why a concern is brought to the table must be considered. Be sure it is for the purpose of bringing about goodness in the relationship and not evil.

- Both parties must have the opportunity to share their concerns and be heard by the other.

Chapter 2

A CHANGE IN DIRECTION

"So when was the last time you guys decided to have a good fight?" Mike questioned.

"What do you mean?" asked Jake. "I don't think we *ever* just decide to fight—probably the opposite. I hate to fight and usually choose *not* to fight."

"Okay," Mike smiled, "so that was kind of a trick question. Very few people decide to have a fight—it just happens. That means you have to know the right thing to do and even practice it before the fight occurs. Doing so will enable you to respond well. A paramedic friend of mine once shared about how thoroughly they are trained. When the real emergency happens, he doesn't stop to think through the steps to take. He doesn't have time. He relies on his instinct that stems from the long hours of training.

"In the same way, you must be prepared to handle conflict when it suddenly comes upon you. Unfortunately, very few people grow up in a home where parents teach or model how to process conflict in a healthy or loving manner. My goal in our time together is to give you the needed preparation. Hopefully as a result, you will avoid what most often happens in a conflict. Typically, one or both parties is hurt through fighting. Or someone makes the choice to not say anything, which causes the issue to go underground. Eventually however, it erupts like a geyser, leading to more pain in the end."

"Wow," said Lisa, "I'd say we've got both of those in our marriage—I'm the fighter, and he's the geyser!"

"Neither work well—do they?" Mike quickly added, "There has to be another way—a way to not only work through our frustrations with each other, but also to learn from the experience and love each other well. Make sense?"

Jake and Lisa looked at each other, then nodded.

"Okay," Mike spoke enthusiastically. "Let's dig in. I am going to teach you a very practical method to process conflict. As I said earlier, this method will enable you to not only resolve conflict, but learn from it at the same time. To teach the method, I use the word PLEDGE as an acronym. It will be a guide to take you through the six steps I will teach you. It will also serve as a reminder. Jake and Lisa—when you got married, you *pledged* to love each other until you parted in death, right?"

"We did."

"Good. From this point on, whenever you experience conflict at any level, I want you to remember that pledge! I want you to remember your pledge to love each other well for life—and now also to PLEDGE your way through conflict, okay?"

They nodded. Lisa began digging in her purse. She pulled out her planner, found a blank page, and then, raising her eyebrows to ask permission, she leaned over to snag a pen off of Mike's desk, which was sitting a little to her right. Then she turned back to face Mike as he turned back to the whiteboard.

"I'll start with a quick overview of the process, and then we'll break it down and talk in detail about each step," Mike said as he wrote the word "PLEDGE" vertically in big letters. "The six steps represented by PLEDGE are Pause, Listen, Echo, Disarm, Give, and Engage. Each of these steps must take place in a conversation if the conflict is to have any real hope of getting resolved. Also, as we go through this, keep in mind that the steps must be implemented in the exact order they are listed.

"When a conflict happens," Mike began, "you have to *Pause* to let your emotions dial down and get your heart prepared to think of each other first. It will also give you time to think about what you're going to say, increasing the chances that you'll do more good than harm. And when you do talk, someone has to volunteer first to *Listen*. It doesn't work very well when you're both talking at the same time! Jake, let's say you decide to be the one who *Listens* first. After doing so, you must *Echo* back what you heard Lisa say to make sure you heard correctly. And once you are assured that you did, you move to the next step—*Disarm*. This is a matter of validating what Lisa said. Once she truly feels heard and understood, you move to the fifth step, *Give*. This step starts off with you being quiet. You just validated what Lisa said, and now you get quiet. You wait until she *Gives* you the chance to share your perspective next. And when she does, you both *Engage* the process all over again, only this time you switch roles. Finally, you keep *Engaging* this cycle over and over until either the conflict is resolved, or you both truly appreciate each other's perspective. In this way you will be at a better place to make a decision and move forward together." He capped his marker and asked, "Simple enough?"

Lisa scribbled a few more words. "I think so."

"I'm not sure," said Jake, eyeing her rapid pen.

Mike smiled as he sat back down. "No problem—as I said that's the overview. We'll go into more detail and then practice to make sure you both understand, okay?"

"Okay, so we start with the first step," Jake sneaked a peek at Lisa's notes, "which is, um, Pause."

Chapter 2 Highlights

- You must be prepared in advance, to work through conflict in a healthy and loving manner.
- You pledged to love each other until "death do you part"; now you must PLEDGE your way through conflict:
    - **Pause** to dial down your emotions, think about what you want to say, and get your heart in the right position
    - **Listen** to understand
    - **Echo** what was said
    - **Disarm** through validating each other's perspective
    - **Give** each other a chance to share
    - **Engage** this process over and over

Chapter 3

DIALING DOWN AND SHIFTING FOCUS

"Starting a quarrel is like opening a floodgate, so stop before a dispute breaks out."
~ Proverbs 17:14 (New International Version)

Mike started with, "When you find yourselves in the middle of a conflict and emotions are rising—someone has to hit the Pause button before any further damage takes place in the relationship. Now, I know that's kind of a no-brainer. I think most people would easily agree this is a wise step. But, over and over again when I teach this to couples, I hear them say, 'That sounds good, but it's not something we do!' Why do you think people don't hit the Pause button?"

Lisa spoke up right away, "If something's on my mind, I want to get it out before I forget it. If it's what I'm feeling, I tell him!"

"And when she does, I shut down," Jake admitted.

"You do—every time!" Lisa quickly interjected. "That's why I come away feeling like you never listen!"

"Jake, why do you think you shut down?" Mike asked.

"She says so much, I just can't keep it all straight. I start feeling pressure with everything there is to talk about. It's also the way she says it. It's like she hates me or something!"

"I don't hate you!" reacted Lisa.

"Well, sometimes it sure feels like it!" Jake shot back.

Speaking in a Way that Can Be Heard

"Okay—let's stop a minute," Mike quickly jumped in, trying to stay on top of the conversation. "Earlier in our session, we talked about how one of the important aspects of good communication is that we say things in a way that can be heard. Lisa, Jake just mentioned that the way you say things sometimes causes him to shut down. What do you think about that?"

"It's confusing. On the one hand it makes sense, but on the other hand—what am I supposed to do, Mike, when I have all these feelings inside? Pretend they don't exist? That's what I feel like you're asking; either that, or I treat him like a wimp who can't take what I have to say!"

Yikes, Mike thought, *here we go again.* That last sentence had some real bite to it, and Mike was sure Jake felt the sting of it.

"Lisa, I can appreciate what you're saying and how it is confusing. Can I share with you what I mean?" asked Mike.

"Fine," she said, still a little irritated.

"Thanks," replied Mike. "First, I don't ever want someone to hear me saying you need to pretend your feelings don't exist—because that simply isn't true. They are a very real part of who you are. I also wouldn't want to communicate that you must go around viewing others as wimps and treating them as such. That only breeds contempt in both parties. At the same time, I want you to consider the meaning of this proverb: 'Death and life are in the power of the tongue[1].' Think about that for a moment, and tell me what comes to mind."

Looking a little guilty over her earlier words, Lisa quietly said, "Ouch. Okay. I get it. How I say something to Jake *does* matter. But I still don't know what to do with all my feelings when I'm talking with him."

Mike took up the opportunity for further instruction. "Here's my suggestion: choose to put your feelings aside for a bit. Imagine sticking them up on a nearby shelf. That way they're out of your focus—but not out of your reach. There will come a time in the conversation when you take your thoughts and feelings back down and share them with Jake. It's vitally important, however, that you do that at the right time. Remember when I introduced the steps of PLEDGE? I said they *must* be taken in the exact order that I teach them.

---

[1] Proverbs 18:21a (NKJV)

You'll learn the appropriate time to share your feelings as we go along. For now, keep in mind the challenge of the proverb. When you share what's on your mind, be careful to do so in a way that brings life to him and to your relationship rather than death. Does that make sense, Lisa?"

"It does. I need to think about it a bit, but it makes sense."

"Okay, good. So to get back on track, we were talking about why we don't usually hit the Pause button when we find ourselves in the midst of a conflict. Apart from just wanting to vent your feelings, what else might keep you from hitting Pause?"

Jake leaned forward. "For me, I just want to get my points in while I can. I watch for when she takes a breath and then I'm in!" He said this with a small grin on his face as he glanced at Lisa. She rolled her eyes with a half-smile and shook her head.

"Sure. We tend to take our shots when we can," Mike agreed.

"I guess, too," Jake said, "I kind of bottle things up inside—when she goes on and on like she does. I do shut down—but only at first. Eventually I can't take it anymore, and I react." He glanced at Lisa apologetically, "That's when I sort of explode and tell her where she needs to get off."

"And then when he goes off—that really hurts me! It scares me, too, sometimes." Lisa suddenly grew quiet as she mulled over what she just said. When she spoke again, she was more subdued. "I guess what he says and how he says it can bring death to me, too."

The Importance of Focus

"That's a good observation, Lisa," Mike agreed soberly. After a few moments, he asked, "What would it look like to bring life through our words instead of death?"

Jake cleared his throat. "It would mean to stop focusing on myself."

A little surprised by his ready and thoughtful answer, Mike asked, "How so?"

"Well, I was just thinking, all my reasons for not hitting the Pause button are all about me. I want to get my points in before she does. I was hurt by what she said. I feel like it's my right to tell her what I think. Or I just flat out don't care!" Jake cleared his throat. "If I want my words to bring life to Lisa, my focus has to be on her."

Lisa's eyes filled with tears as she heard all this from her usually uncommunicative husband. She blinked rapidly and looked down at her hands.

Mike smiled, "Wow, Jake—you hit the nail on the head there. If we want to have good communication with each other, and especially if we ever hope to be able to work through conflict well, our focus can't be on ourselves—it has to be on the other person!"

"That's true," Lisa said softly.

"It is, but it's so contrary to the way most people relate to each other. How often in any conversation, for instance, do you sense people thinking of others more than themselves?" Mike asked with the sound of frustration in his voice.

"Almost never," Jake said slowly. "I think that's why I don't like to talk much to people. Everyone's just so quick to jump in with their point rather than pay attention to what they just heard. Like when someone has a joke or story to share, almost before they're even finished, someone else speaks up to tell *their* story. Most of the time I just blow it off, but when I stop and think about it, it's kind of annoying."

"And sad," Mike added, "because we miss the opportunity to really reflect on what someone else has shared. And what's even more sad is that we miss the opportunity to affirm the person who did the sharing. Affirmation is something we all long for, but rarely experience from others."

"Because most people, myself included, don't really think much about giving it to others," Jake replied.

Jake was getting it. *That's an encouraging sign*, Mike thought.

"There is one more reason we don't hit the Pause button when a conflict emerges," Mike added. "Lisa, usually women think of this reason. Any ideas?"

"I don't really know. When I start talking about something important to me though, I know I feel like I can't stop. I think I'm afraid if I do, we'll never get it resolved. So that could be something that keeps me from hitting the Pause button—or from letting Jake hit it, too. In fact, I usually get angry when he says, 'Let's talk about this later'!"

"That's it, Lisa. Often a spouse fears the concern will never again be discussed. They assume it will be swept under the already bulging carpet, only to be tripped over again at a later time. So this is what I tell people: when one spouse feels the

Dialing Down and Shifting Focus

need to Pause, both must agree to do so. Often one spouse wants to Pause and the other doesn't. The one who doesn't want to may even accuse the other of just trying to avoid the situation. That may or may not be true. That's why I also say that when the Pause button is hit, both people must agree on a time to come back and talk through the conflict using the rest of PLEDGE. It may be two minutes, two hours, or two days, but you agree to come back."

"What determines the length of time?" asked Lisa.

"Well, other than circumstantial elements like each other's schedules, it depends mainly on one critical factor. Jake spoke of it earlier—it has to do with focus. You come back to the table when a shift has taken place in your heart from a focus on yourself to that of your spouse. If this all-important shift has not taken place, you will not be prepared to move on to the next step of PLEDGE."

"And what was that again?" asked Jake.

Lisa glanced at her notes. "It's called Listen."

Chapter 3 Highlights

- When in the midst of conflict, you must hit the Pause button to avoid any further damage.

- Reasons why you might not want to hit the Pause button:
  - Wanting to say what is on your mind before you forget.
  - Wanting to get your point across the moment you can.
  - Wanting to say something hurtful.
  - Feeling you have a right to say what is on your mind or what you feel.
  - Being afraid that if you don't talk about it now, it may never get talked about.

- The main purpose for the Pause step is for both of you to dial down your emotions and to prepare your heart and mind to reengage the conversation with a focus on the other person rather than on yourselves.

- When someone hits the Pause button, both must agree on a time when you will reconvene to continue the dialogue.

- What ultimately determines the length of the Pause is the amount of time it takes for both of you to shift your heart's focus—thinking first of the other person. It could be two minutes, two hours, or two days.

Chapter 4

DISCOVERING THE HEART OF THE OTHER

"Let the wise listen, and add to their learning…" - Proverbs 1:5 (NIV)

"The next step in the process of PLEDGE is to Listen," Mike explained. "This will not be done well unless the focus of the person Listening is consciously shifted to the other person."

"Makes sense," said Jake. "Kind of hard to do, though. I'm not sure I really know how to make that shift stick. I could see myself trying and quickly ending up reacting again. That's probably why I usually just walk away without even trying. I just get caught up in my own feelings and thoughts."

"I understand, Jake. It *is* hard to shift our focus," Mike concurred, "especially when we're so full of emotions or harboring resentment. It is, however, a step that must be taken. Research shows that even low levels of anger impair our abilities to solve problems.[2] Anger has a way of causing us to narrow our thinking. We tend to see things one way only—our way. And that will not help when we're in the midst of a conflict.

"It's while Pausing," Mike reminded them, "that you must find a way to shift your focus from yourself to your spouse, so that you can truly Listen to them. Then you'll be able to continue with the rest of the PLEDGE process."

"I can see that, Mike—but how? How do you do that when you're so full of anger or hurt or bitterness?" asked Lisa.

"That's a tough one, Lisa. All I can do is tell you how I do it."

"Okay," she said, a little dubiously.

Helps for Shifting Focus

Mike rubbed the back of his head thoughtfully. "If I'm going to make the shift in my heart, it really starts with honesty. I have to be completely honest with myself about what I'm feeling and why. This is easier for some than it is for others. Some people have a very difficult time knowing what it is

---

[2] "Anger and Health." *CompassionPower.com.* CompassionPower, n.d. Web. 29 Sept. 2013. <http://compassionpower.com/Angerand Health.php>.

they're feeling, let alone why. When that's the case, there are a few things you can do."

Thinking out loud, Mike continued, "I am big on journaling—even if you just write something down and then throw it away. Take a piece of paper and start writing anything and everything that comes to mind about what's going on inside you and why. Write down as best as you can what you are feeling. When did the feelings start? Where might they have come from? What do you think they're caused by? What thoughts come with them?"

Lisa glanced down at her little planner with the cramped notes she had been writing down so far. "I think that might be a good method for me," she chuckled.

"Another thing to do is to get with a trusted friend and talk about what's going on inside. Understand what I mean by a trusted friend, though. You have to find someone who's going to listen and draw you out. This person needs to ask you questions to help you sort out what's going on inside. That is the biggest part they need to play. Don't look for someone who will just 'feel your pain' and agree with you on everything. That person will only increase your focus on self. Also, don't go to someone who just wants to give you easy answers. That person will keep you from being deeply honest and from exploring what's going on inside. Remember, that's where you need to start—being completely honest with yourself about what you're feeling and why."

"Huh," Jake broke in, "I've never thought about having a friend who would do that. I'm not sure I have a friend like that. The guys at work and church that I usually hang out with…

well, I'm pretty sure they'd just be the 'I feel your pain, man' type. Well, except for Todd," he mused, "but I think he'd just give me a bunch of philosophical answers."

Mike nodded sympathetically. "It takes some work to have that kind of relationship, and you do have to be intentional about it. To find such a friend, you might look for an older man who is wise and has a good marriage. Then tell him what you're looking for—someone you can turn to at times to listen to you when you need to sort things out. Tell him straight up that you won't be looking so much for answers from him but questions that will help you be honest in exploring what it is you're feeling and why."

"You know, I think I know someone like that. I'll probably see him on Sunday. Maybe I'll talk with him then and see what he says."

"Good, Jake. I'm glad. Okay, so once you've found a way to identify your feelings—and there are definitely more ways than the ones I've just mentioned—the next thing to do is to spend some time in reflection. I usually start by thinking about the person I'm upset with. I think about how I really feel about them at the core of my being. If it's my wife, for instance, I think about how, deep inside, I know I really love her and appreciate her. And I remind myself of all the reasons why. I tell myself that I'm sure, in the core of *her* being, she loves me, too. No doubt, whatever she did that hurt or angered me probably didn't come out of the deepest part of her. More likely they came out of the surface part of her that reacts quickly to hurtful or upsetting things said or done to her. I think about how that is true of me as well."

Jake nodded slowly.

Mike reflected further, "I also spend some time thinking of how I contributed to the situation and made it worse—things I did wrong in the process. I think of what I need to acknowledge to my wife as wrong on my part and apologize. And I recall to mind the pledge I made to her almost 30 years ago when we stood at the altar together. I cannot forget that. I must not forget that—*ever!* For it's that commitment we made to each other that causes me to do what seems impossible in those moments of anger and hurt. That pledge at the altar propels me to move forward and once again put her first in my mind. It's what enables me to shift my focus from myself to her."

Mike paused for a few moments. Both Jake and Lisa were looking thoughtful. He hoped that even now they were starting to make that shift in their own hearts.

Mike took a breath, spreading his hands out before him. "And through it all, I pray. You see, I'm not always aware of everything taking place inside of me, nor do I understand it all. I don't see things as clearly as I need to from just thinking about them myself. I need help. So do you. One source of help I regularly turn to is God. Either in writing, or out loud, or in my head, I ask Him for help. When I'm real with God, He helps me to see things more clearly about myself or the situation. And oftentimes, it's not pretty. I'll see attitudes in myself that are just… well, bad. I'll see how I could have done things differently. I could have been more kind or patient or helpful. Honestly reflecting on those things usually has the effect of reducing my anger and hurt. And the focus of my heart begins to shift—I can feel it happening.

"Also, maybe what I heard my wife say wasn't really what she meant to say or meant me to hear. Maybe she just had a really bad day. I know I have bad days and say things or react to people in ways that I later regret. Maybe something deeper is happening inside her or in our relationship that we need to get out in the open and discuss. I don't know. Any or all of the above could be happening. The important thing is that this shift takes place in my heart where I'm willing to lay everything I think and feel aside—at least temporarily—in order to listen well and understand the heart of my wife. And for this to happen, I am very aware I need God. As hard as I try to deal with my own emotions or perspectives, I can't seem to do it well on my own. I need a nudge from the outside to get me moving in the right direction—and for me, that nudge is God."

Jake was beginning to look a little overwhelmed, but Lisa wanted to know more. "And when that all happens, then what?"

"When I make the shift to put my wife first," Mike responded, "that's when I'm able to come back to our conversation. It's like this: before I hit the Pause button, I'm primarily focused on what *I* am feeling and thinking. I'm centered mostly on myself. By taking time to pause and pray, I'm ultimately reminded of my unconditional vow to love. It is then that I'm able to come back to the table, putting my focus on my wife. I come back to listen—to really *Listen* to what she has to say."

"Makes sense," said Lisa.

Jake sighed. "Sounds like a lot of work."

"Actually Jake, we're just getting started!" Mike grinned. "I agree, though. It is a lot of work. But look at it this way. The work you do up front in this process will save you a great deal more work in the end. It's kind of like doing your taxes. You can save your receipts every day, record your expenses, and keep track of your records all year long—or do it all at the end of the year. Which is going to be easier?"

"It's funny you should mention taxes," Lisa said wryly. "We have gone both routes—but more often the latter. In fact, we have to go home and sort our taxes out this weekend because this is one of those times when we've put it off as long as we can."

"Yeah," said Jake, running his hand through his hair. "And I'm *not* looking forward to it—it always ends up being so stressful and frustrating. Come tax time, I always tell myself it would be so much easier if we had kept things up all year. But we keep finding ourselves again in the same mess."

Lisa, looking annoyed, opened her mouth to say something then changed her mind.

Mike sensed the tension beginning to build again, so he continued with, "Unfortunately, that's the mess people often find themselves in with their relationships. They don't take the time, or they don't know how, to work on issues between them all along the way. And suddenly, the problems they face seem overwhelming, and trying to sort everything out feels impossible. Their resolve to do whatever it takes disappears, and then giving up becomes their only option."

"I hope we never get to that point," said Lisa.

"Good!" exclaimed Mike. "Well, let's get back to talking about PLEDGE. A conflict happens, big or small, and the first thing you need to do is Pause—to dial down your emotions and get your hearts in the right place so you can truly focus on each other rather than yourselves."

The Challenge of Listening

Mike gave that a few moments to sink in and went on, "When you're ready to come back to the table, someone has to volunteer to take the next step first—that of Listening. My recommendation is that whoever hit the Pause button first is the one who volunteers to Listen first. This isn't a hard and fast rule but a general principle. The one who initially says, 'Let's Pause,' usually is the one to have the emotional resources and self-control to carry out the next steps in the most loving manner. They are more likely to be able to Listen well.

"So Jake, let's say you hit the Pause button first. You both agree to take a break and come back at a later time to talk through the issue. During that time, you both engage in the exercise I just talked about. Now you're back and, Jake, you volunteer first to Listen. Here is what you must keep in mind. The tendency of most of us when we're listening, particularly in a conflict, is to listen only long enough for us to build our line of defense. Then we wait—and the moment the other person takes a long enough breath, we go in for the kill! In one way or another, we tell them why they're wrong and we're right. Well, as you can imagine, this doesn't go over very well."

Discovering the Heart of the Other

"You can say that again!" said Jake. "And I don't even have to imagine it. That's what happens all the time with us."

"I think we both do that," Lisa quickly added. "Although if I'm honest, I might even do it more than Jake. It's like I can't stop myself from telling him where he's wrong. I think I'm afraid that if I don't jump in right away to correct him, he'll think I agree with him. And oftentimes I don't! So I need to tell him before I forget, or he'll get the wrong idea."

"And Lisa, while at first that seems to make the most sense, my guess is it rarely helps, but only makes matters worse. Am I right?" Mike asked.

Lisa nodded, saying, "When I jump in to tell him what I think, he just interrupts me in the same way, and then we're off to the races—each of us trying to outdo the other. And it usually gets ugly."

"Here is what you need to learn to do instead, Lisa, and you as well, Jake," said Mike. "You have to put yourself in Listening mode to learn, to discover, and to understand—*not* to defend! You must put all your thoughts, feelings, and reactions on the shelf—for now—and shift your focus toward your spouse. You must focus on learning all you can about their perspective. As you Listen, you may ask questions, but *only* to further understand or clarify what is being said. The goal, remember, is to discover their perspective and understand their heart. Keep in mind: they reacted the way they did because of something. They thought, they said, and they did what they did for a reason. Your primary task is to learn why.

"Are you with me? Am I making sense?" Mike quizzed them both.

They nodded silently.

"Good. Let me emphasize again one part of what I just said. When you're Listening to your spouse, and particularly when you're working through a conflict, you have to work hard not to defend yourself but to understand the other person's heart. That means you let all kinds of words and tones of voice fly past you as you focus on the core message they want you to hear.

"Let me give you guys an example," Mike went on. "As you have probably noticed by now, there are some real differences between the two of you—and I don't just mean male and female."

"You can say that again," Jake quickly muttered, rolling his eyes. All three chuckled.

Mike continued with his point, "Because of these differences, we often don't understand each other. I have no doubt that every husband and wife at one point or another has at least thought to themselves or said out loud to the other, 'You just don't get it!'"

Lisa blushed slightly at this. There were many times she had said those very words to her husband.

"Now here's my question. Jake, if Lisa says that to you, what do you do next? Think about it. The moment is filled with all kinds of explosive possibilities. Your response is critical. What you do will determine whether things erupt or dial down."

Mike's question had clearly captured Jake's attention. "I don't know. What *should* I do?"

"Well, I can't tell you exactly," replied Mike, "because every situation is a little different. But I can tell you if there was ever a moment in conversation when you ought to hit the Pause button, that would be it. You and I both know if our wife made that comment to us, our first tendency would be to react. We would most likely say something that would only exacerbate the problem. Instead, you Pause and get quiet—for the very reasons I have been explaining. You have to let her words fly by, so to speak, while *you* make sure your emotions are under control."

"That sounds hard," said Lisa, with Jake nodding in agreement. "It certainly isn't how I'm prone to go about it when he's upset with me—but it makes sense."

"Good," said Mike. "Back to you now, Jake. At some point, you have to get back into the dialogue and seek to understand the cry of Lisa's heart. She said what she did for *some* reason. Your job is to ask why."

"Wow," muttered Jake. "That's a bit scary. There's no telling what she'll say next!"

"It is scary," Mike agreed. "That's why what I'm suggesting rarely happens. Most people either react in anger or throw their hands up in the air and walk away. Neither of those responses is motivated by love, whereas my suggestion is."

"Okay," said Jake, clearly in thought over the whole idea. "Anything else?"

"Yes. When your heart is ready, you rise up to the occasion and ask her to tell you what was behind her words. Why did she say them? What does she want you to understand that somehow you've missed? And when she talks, you do your absolute best at Listening: to learn, to discover, and to understand her heart.

"Keep in mind, as you said earlier, Jake, it will be a little scary. You *don't* know what Lisa will say next. But if you stay in the posture of Listening—to hear her heart—eventually her emotions will dial down, and she'll begin to feel like maybe you really do care."

"That would be amazing!" Lisa exclaimed. "If he would really do that, I would be stunned! Don't get me wrong, I would love it, but I would be stunned."

"As you just said, Lisa, you would feel loved. That's the goal, remember?" Mike commented as he looked at them both with a twinkle in his eyes.

"So, Jake," Mike summed up, "once you believe you have correctly heard what is in Lisa's heart, then you are ready for the next step of PLEDGE."

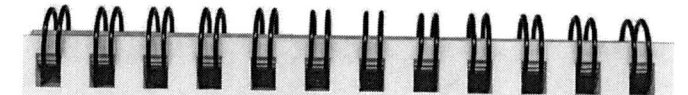

Chapter 4 Highlights

- You can Listen well only when you have consciously shifted your focus to the other person.
- To shift your focus:
    - You must be honest with yourself about what you are feeling and why.
    - Journal or ask a trusted friend to help you.
    - Spend time reflecting on what you appreciate about your spouse; consider also how you contributed to the situation.
    - Remember the pledge you made to your spouse at the altar.
    - Now remember your PLEDGE to love your spouse through conflict and put him/her first in your mind.
    - Ask God to reveal anything further you need to see.
- Come back to the table ready to Listen—usually the person who hit the Pause button volunteers to Listen first.
- Listen to learn, discover, and understand—not defend.
- The goal is to understand the heart of your spouse.

Chapter 5

A CRITICAL BUT FORGOTTEN STEP

*"The heart of the discerning acquires knowledge,
for the ears of the wise seek it out."*
~ Proverbs 18:15 (NIV)

"Okay, we are on to step three—" Mike's voice cracked, hoarse from so much talking. He paused a moment to clear his throat. While he did so, Jake excused himself to step outside briefly and came back balancing three plastic cups of water from the water dispenser in the hall. He gave one each to Mike and Lisa and then sat back down on the couch.

"Thanks, Jake," Mike smiled gratefully as Lisa added her thanks. Mike took a drink, then balanced the cup on the arm of his chair and picked up where he had left off. "Okay, so the third step of PLEDGE is Echo. When you think you have fully heard what your spouse has said—and you believe you understand their perspective and their heart—you Echo it back to see if you heard correctly."

"Meaning what exactly?" asked Jake.

"Meaning, quite literally, repeat back as closely as you can what the other person just said. Often when it comes time to do this, we fall short. We thought we were listening well, but when it comes time to Echo back we can't—or at least not as well as we thought. When this happens, you must ask the other person to repeat what they said while you Listen and Echo back once again.

Four Reasons

"There are four reasons it is critical to Echo back what you heard," Mike continued. "First, as I just alluded to, it allows you to find out if you've heard everything correctly. It's amazing how you think you know exactly what a person said, but when you Echo it back, you find out otherwise. It can be a frustrating experience. Do you remember when I talked about the importance of preparing ahead of time, before conflict ever occurs?"

Both nodded their heads.

"Every day in every conversation," Mike instructed, "I want you to ask yourself, 'How well am I listening to what the other person has to say? What's going through my mind while they're talking? Am I thinking of my response or reflecting on what they're saying?' Then, Echo back to them what you

A Critical but Forgotten Step

heard them say and ask if it was correct. You may be surprised. This is not only a great exercise in preparation but a good way to improve all your conversations and relationships. And it will train you well for when you find yourself in the midst of a conflict."

"Interesting," Jake said. "When I think of training, I think back to my years in basketball. We would train for hours with drills, plays, different shots, passing—everything—so when it was time for the game, we knew what to do and did it right. If Lisa and I trained hard to communicate and work through conflict *before* it happened, man, that could make a huge difference!"

Lisa was dumbfounded. Was that her husband talking? Was he really taking all this in as he seemed to be?

Mike smiled. "Great comparison, Jake. And I totally believe you're right. I would even go a bit further. You could look at every conversation as an opportunity not only for personal training but to affirm and encourage others—all of which would prepare you for talking with your spouse, particularly in regard to difficult subject matters."

Mike took a breath, "Okay, so the first reason to Echo back is to find out if you have heard correctly. The second is similar. It allows the *speaker* to know whether or not the listener heard correctly. It's true for all of us—when we speak, we want to know if we're being heard. When someone echoes back, we know they were listening, and we also find out if they understood what we said."

Lisa hurriedly turned to another page to keep taking notes.

"Here is the third reason to Echo: if you know you're going to have to Echo what you've heard, it forces you to shift your focus from yourself to the other person. This step is like a built-in mechanism to help you make and maintain that shift. It is impossible to fully Listen if your primary focus is still on your own feelings, thoughts, and reactions. Only when your focus is largely on the other person are you able to concentrate enough to hear clearly what they are saying. Knowing you will have to Echo back forces you to Listen well."

"I think this will really help both of us," Lisa interrupted. "It will help us stop the volleying back and forth that we talked about earlier."

Mike chuckled. "You actually jumped ahead of me there to my fourth reason."

"Oh, sorry," she said, a little embarrassed.

"That's fine. But yes, when you Echo, it slows down the interaction between you. In essence, as you just said, Lisa, it stops the volleying back and forth. This enables you to have more control over your emotions. Now, hear me carefully on this. I'm *not* saying you should stuff your emotions, but I *am* saying you cannot be ruled by them. When your emotions begin to skyrocket, rational thinking basically goes out the window—which almost guarantees the conversation is not going to be profitable. If you find this happening, simply loop back to the beginning and hit Pause again. Then pick up where you left off when you're more able to focus your listening on your spouse. Keep in mind, the time to Pause might need to be of some length, or it could be a matter of only 30 seconds.

A Critical but Forgotten Step

The task is to get your focus off of self and back on to the other. As soon as you do, you can proceed."

Mike stopped for another sip of water. Lisa kept writing, and Jake looked like he was doing some serious thinking.

"Okay, any questions on the third step?" Mike smiled slyly and added, "Can either of you *Echo* back what I just said?"

Jake snorted, "You just said a lot, but I think I've got the gist: after we Listen to what the other person has to say, we repeat back what they've said to make sure we heard it all and understand it."

"And why is this step important?" Mike prodded.

As Jake floundered a bit, Lisa scanned her notes and replied with the four reasons Mike had just explained to them.

"Very good," said Mike. He glanced at his watch. "Well, it looks like our hour together is winding down. You two have done a great job of listening—and even taking notes." He grinned at Lisa's hodgepodge of scribbled bullet points and arrows. "But before we finish up, give me some feedback—what strikes you about the step we call Echo?"

Jake spoke up first. "I think this step may be especially difficult for me. When Lisa gets to talking, she goes on and on and on. I'm afraid I'll never remember everything she says to Echo it back to her. What do I do when that happens?"

"Great question, Jake. Here are a few thoughts. Don't be afraid to grab a paper and pen and jot down a few of her key points to help you remember. That will help you to Echo back what she's saying. Sometimes we think doing something like that is dumb or reveals our weaknesses. I say, if it helps the conversation—and therefore the relationship—do it!

"Secondly, and this is for you, Lisa—learn to talk through a subject in bite-sized pieces. A person can only remember so much! So take one point to discuss at a time.

"Now back to you one more time, Jake. When Listening to Lisa, if you find yourself losing the ability to follow her, gently interrupt her and ask if you can Echo back what you have heard so far. That will signal to her that she was losing you and give you an opportunity to stay as close as possible to what she is saying."

"Huh—that's good," reflected Jake. "I could see doing that—as long as Lisa is okay with me interrupting her. I'm afraid she might react and think I'm not trying hard enough to listen."

"You know," responded Lisa, "I think if you had done that in the past, Jake, I might have thought that, but now that I see what I'm doing and we're learning this new way of communicating, I think I would be okay with you interrupting me—as long as you do it in a careful way, as Mike said." She looked a little sheepish as she added, "I know I do have a tendency to go on and on, which would make it difficult for you to Echo back—so you stopping me periodically would probably be good."

"Good for both of you," Mike jumped in. "I'm excited to see how you're already interacting better with each other. Is there anything else either of you would want to comment on regarding Echo?"

"I really like the concept of Echo for one main reason," said Lisa. "When I'm sharing with Jake what I'm feeling, I want to know if he's really listening... and if he really gets what

A Critical but Forgotten Step

I'm saying. If he can Echo back to me what I say, that would be wonderful. Then I'd know for sure we're on the same page."

"Yes—and that's actually true for all of us, Lisa. Whenever any one of us speaks—we want to know we're being listened to. It's that simple… and yet so important. Knowing we're being listened to is paramount to good communication," Mike said to them both.

"Okay—here's my thinking at this point. We still have three more steps of PLEDGE to discuss, but I want to take a break and let you practice what you have learned so far. I've written out an assignment on the first three steps that I want you to do every day between now and when we meet again." He got up and walked over to his desk, reached into a drawer, and pulled out a sheet of paper for each of them. "Read through this and see if you have any questions."

PLEDGE Practice Assignment

The purpose of this exercise is to help you sift through what you have learned about the first three steps of PLEDGE: Pause, Listen, and Echo. If you are truly going to learn how to communicate well, especially when in conflict, you will have to wrestle with the concepts to make sure you understand them and know what it takes to put them into action. Between today and our next session, please practice the following:

1. On a daily basis, as often as you remember in everyday conversation, think:

   - **PAUSE**: Every word out of my mouth can bring death or life to the person in front of me. I want to love well and bring forth life. Therefore, I will not just say the first thing that comes to mind. Instead, I will work at evaluating what I am about to say and only choose words that seek to build our relationship. This will take work. It will require that I shift my focus from myself to the person in front of me. It will not be easy. I will be stretched in the process. By doing this, however, I will be learning how to love well.

   - **LISTEN**: When someone is talking to me, I will work hard to fully understand what they are saying and Listen to the heart behind their words. I may gently interrupt to clarify a point or see if I am still tracking with them but not to correct them or defend myself.

   - **ECHO**: When they are done talking, I will check to see if I understand them by Echoing back what I have heard and asking them if I heard correctly.

2. When conflicts arise, big or small, go through the above steps—knowing you will have to work hard at the process if you are to communicate and love well.

A Critical but Forgotten Step

"Okay, do either of you have any questions about the assignment?" asked Mike.

"So we're supposed to do all these steps with everyone we talk to, not just each other?" Jake wondered, looking a bit confused.

"Yes. That will help you think about and practice the steps all the time. It's better than waiting for a conflict to arise between you and Lisa and *then* trying to remember and implement the steps. That isn't likely to be very successful. Think of this like the basketball practice before the game that you talked about earlier."

Jake nodded his understanding.

"Lisa? Any last thoughts or questions?"

"Nope. I think this all has been very helpful."

"Good. I think you both are taking steps in the right direction." Mike thought of one more thing to mention to them, "Remember, as you're working through PLEDGE this week, it's one thing to talk about the steps here in my office, but it's another thing entirely to practice them on your own. Things probably won't go as smoothly as you hope right off the bat, and you may really struggle with changing the patterns of communication you've developed over your last 15 years of marriage. If you keep working at it, though, you will get better—and so will your relationship."

Mike checked his schedule book and said, "It looks like you're scheduled to come back in a week. We'll go over the last three steps of PLEDGE then. I'll look forward to hearing how things go for you this next week!"

Jake and Lisa murmured their agreement and gathered up their things. They thanked him for their time together and then headed out of the office to their car.

As he watched them go, Mike was energized as he felt that both Jake and Lisa were eager to learn. They were quick to see why their efforts in the past had failed and willing to adopt new ways of relating and work at bringing them to pass. They likely would struggle more than they realized now, but with time and practice, they would experience a growing measure of success. Eventually it would become a part of their everyday way of relating.

Chapter 5 Highlights

- When you think you have heard what your spouse said—and you believe you understand their perspective and heart—Echo it back to them to see if you heard correctly. If not, ask them to repeat what they said and try again.
- Four reasons to Echo back:
  - It allows the listener to find out if they have heard everything correctly.
  - It allows the speaker to know whether or not the listener heard correctly.
  - It forces you to shift your focus from yourself to the other person.
  - It slows down the interaction between you both.
- When Listening, don't be afraid to use a paper and pen to jot down key points of what the other says in preparation for Echoing them back.
- Talk through a subject in bite-sized pieces so the listener can follow you.
- Gently interrupt the one talking if you get lost or need them to repeat something.

Putting It into Practice

Chapter 6

KEEPING PERSPECTIVE

As Mike left his office, he stepped out into the warm, heavy air that often preceded a spring thunderstorm. He could see clouds building on the horizon and remembered the weatherman warning of severe weather that evening, with hail and tornadoes possible. Keeping an eye on the sky and an ear alert for the siren that would signal a tornado warning, he hurried to the parking lot. He got into his car and closed the door, thankful that home was just a few minutes away.

As he turned onto the street, he thought to himself how refreshing it was to meet with a couple like Jake and Lisa. Most couples he worked with had such cold hearts. He thought of the difficulties couples face as they go through different seasons in life and are confronted by the winds of adversity. He clenched his jaw and shook his head—as much from the pain-filled stories he had heard from other couples earlier that day as from the lightning now flashing against the angry sky. It had been a long day. He was eager to get home and relax.

We All Struggle

A mile away from home, the oil light began to flash. Mike had always told his kids to pull off the road immediately if the oil light ever came on or they would risk blowing the engine. He was no mechanic, but he knew you couldn't drive without oil. Mike was driving his wife's car since his own was in the shop. He remembered her car needed oil added to the engine quite regularly. *How many times have I reminded her to make sure the oil level was full? Why doesn't she pay more attention to things like this?*

It was late. He was tired. The weather was getting worse by the minute. And the oil light was on. He knew it would be best to pull over and add oil, but he just wanted to get home. Still, his better judgment won out. He pulled off to the side of the road and popped the trunk to look for oil. "Sure wish I had a flashlight," he thought out loud. He felt around the trunk but didn't find one—nor did he feel any containers of oil. All he could think of was unwinding at home and wishing he were dry rather than being pelted by the cold rain now starting to plunk down all around him. His irritation was swiftly turning into anger.

"I know I put two quarts of oil in the trunk just a few months ago! Why didn't she replace them if she used them?" he growled to himself. He deliberated for a few seconds and decided to go home on foot. It was probably only about ten blocks, but he would have to run to get there before the storm unleashed its full fury. He could have called his wife for a ride but knew she was across town at a friend's home for a baby shower, and anyway, she had driven over with someone else who was going to bring her home afterward. So he closed the trunk, grabbed his wallet and keys, locked the car, and began to jog.

As he ran, his feet immediately began to protest the lack of padding and support in the stiff dress shoes he wore to the office. When a car zipped by him, he thought of how silly he must look running in the rain in slacks and a dress coat. The thunder was sounding closer. The rain and wind grew in intensity. So did his anger. *Not good*, a small part of him said.

It wasn't long before Mike was struggling to catch his breath. He had either miscalculated the number of blocks or overestimated his physical condition when he decided to jog his way home. His thoughts were all over the board. Aware of his increasing frustration and the futility of hoping to get home before he was drenched through, he shot a quick prayer towards the heavens, "Help me, God. Deal with my heart."

God Change Me

When he finally approached the house and panted up the driveway, the automatic porch light came on to illuminate his path. The warm, steady glow cut through the rain and darkness, and a thought sparked in his heart. *Here I am—a marriage counselor—fuming at my wife for something as small as forgetting to put oil in the car.*

He knew Jenny didn't do it on purpose. He knew in her heart she supported him and loved him. So why was he so mad? And how did he get like this as easily as he did sometimes? He taught people every day what it means to love and how it looks in the most practical of ways. He spoke about love requiring people to think of others more than they think of themselves. Yet here he was, angry at his wife.

As Mike unlocked the front door and entered the house, making sure to take off his shoes and dripping coat, he reflected further about how easy it was to lose the focus of love. His out-of-shape breath and heartbeat made him think of Olympic athletes and how hard they worked at keeping their goal in mind. They spent hour after hour, day after day, year after year working to perfect their skills so they might achieve the gold. How often, Mike wondered, did he take seriously the task of perfecting love? Did he even think much about love being something he must work at—every day and every hour? What was the end goal in his life, the ultimate prize when it came to loving his wife and children?

All great questions, he thought. He was stirred and convicted. It was one thing to sit in his office and counsel couples how to love each other well. It was another thing to live it himself day in and day out. Sometimes he felt like such a hypocrite. Then he thought, *Probably a better way of looking at it is that I, too, am still a work in progress. I want to live what I teach others, but the desire to do so isn't always enough to override my own self-centered tendencies, especially when I'm tired.* "Oh

God," he found himself praying, "Change my heart. Help me to be more patient. Help me to be better at looking past the little things that get me so upset at times. Thank you for my wife. I really do love her. Help me to show her that love when she gets home tonight rather than my anger."

The Big Picture

As he sat in his chair to further reflect, his mind went back to the questions he asked himself a few moments ago. With his wife, he knew he wanted to explore the depths of their love for as many years as they would have together. Their experience of love would intensify if they worked at it. He had already known that to be true in their 30 years of marriage thus far. What would it be like if they were blessed to be married 60? He had only met a few who were gifted with that many years together. Mike recalled one such couple, who still truly enjoyed being with each other in their 80s. People just wanted to be around them to watch and listen and learn. He hoped he and Jenny would get there someday.

As for his children, now grown and living on their own, his goal was that he and Jenny would be a light and a hope to them in their marriages. Mike had just recently read a statistic about children of divorced parents. Their one common characteristic was being plagued with fear that their marriage wouldn't work. How could they believe otherwise, when their own parents' marriage had failed?[3] In talking with his kids, Mike recalled many conversations about their friends who grew up with only one parent. He thought of how many children in his wife's third-grade classroom were from homes devastated by divorce. He determined afresh that not only would his children see their home governed by love, but they would be inspired to show others around them that same kind of love.

Mike was so lost in thought that he barely noticed the storm raging outside, slamming wind and hail against the windows. Strangely enough, he found himself thankful for the whole incident with the car. He felt his perspective changing, his anger dissipating, and a new resolve coming over him to love well.

Mike's cell phone rang. When he saw that it was Jenny, he answered immediately, suddenly aware again of the dangerous conditions outside. He was relieved to hear that she was still at her friend's house and had decided to stay there until the worst of the storm had passed. Late that night, when his wife finally arrived home, Mike rejoiced to see her and in his heart gave thanks that she was safe. They were both exhausted, so after a few words of heartfelt thanksgiving that the storm had passed leaving their home unharmed, they went to bed.

The next day over their late-morning Saturday brunch, Mike asked Jenny how yesterday had gone for her and then shared about his day. Mentioning why her car wasn't in the garage, he talked about his drive home the night before, along

---

[3] Wallerstein, Judith S., Julia Lewis, and Sandra Blakeslee, *The Unexpected Legacy of Divorce: A 25 Year Landmark Study* (New York: Hyperion, 2000), (xiii).

with his accompanying anger and reflections afterward. He apologized for how often he got irritated over the little things. She was always so patient with him—and for that he said he was grateful. Rather than say anything more about the oil, he just decided to make it a point for himself every weekend to make sure the oil level was full in her car and extra quarts were in her trunk. Later in the morning, they walked out together to pick up her car.

What began as a very frustrating weekend turned out to be a wonderful time of sharing and growing more in love with each other.

Chapter 7

THE JOURNEY TO HOPE

Jake and Lisa left their counseling session quite hopeful and excited about all they had learned. They barely noticed the storm gathering above them as they began discussing what Mike had taught them. They both agreed to do all they could to put his advice into practice. It was going to be a busy weekend followed by a busy week with their taxes, the children's events, and then work—plenty of opportunity to practice, no doubt.

Testing Is Inevitable

It wasn't long before they were put to the test. Doing their taxes together was always a source of conflict. Neither Jake nor Lisa felt they understood all they should about the process. Jake was supposed to have talked with a friend of his who was an accountant but had forgotten. Lisa was supposed to have kept track of all their receipts throughout the year, but she could only find half of them. Before long, they were both frustrated and making hurtful comments to each other.

Finally, Jake spoke up saying they needed to hit the Pause button and use what they had learned that week with Mike.

Lisa was a bit reluctant to do so, feeling like Jake was just trying to dodge the bullet. "You should have called Matt," she fumed. "Now it's going to take twice as long since we'll have to figure everything out ourselves!"

"I told you I forgot. I didn't do it on purpose! You know how many things are on my plate. I can't do it all!" Jake said in his own defense.

"You *always* forget—at least that's what you say. But you don't forget everything you need to do at work. Everyone *loves* you there because you work so hard and take care of everything. I just wish you took your responsibilities as a husband and father more seriously!" Lisa added more fuel to the fire.

Jake snorted, "You should talk! You say *I'm* irresponsible, but you can't do such a simple thing as keep track of our receipts!"

"Don't even go there! Probably most of the receipts I can't find are yours anyway, because you leave them all over the house or forget to even get them in the first place!"

"That was in the past. It's not true anymore. I give them to you every day now!" Jake paused then sighed. "Lisa, listen—let's stop. Do you see what we're doing to each other again?

We have to stop this and do what Mike asked us to do, or this is only going to get worse!"

Lisa knew Jake was right. She still didn't want to Pause but realized that things would only get worse if they continued. She finally gave way on the strict condition that Jake committed to a specific time to come back to the discussion.

"Okay, fine! How about we try this again at 4:30?" Jake suggested with some exasperation.

Lisa looked at her watch. "That'll be... about two hours." She sighed, frustrated at losing so much time when they needed every hour they had for the work still remaining with their taxes. "Fine, 4:30, then."

Time for Reflection

Jake went out back to chop some wood. His plan was to let it dry over the summer and then sell it when the weather got colder again. Swinging the ax felt good. *Why does she talk to me like that? She always has this tone of condescension—like she has it all together and I don't.*

With each *thunk* of the ax, he found himself replaying in his mind all the times Lisa had wronged him with her words. He knew he couldn't stay angry forever—that wouldn't help things. But it felt good at the moment to defend his own actions to himself... to justify his own thinking... and to mull over how unjust his wife could be at times.

Still, as he stopped to stack the wood he had chopped so far, Jake knew there was some truth to what Lisa was saying. He just didn't want to admit it to himself, let alone to her. He did often feel guilty about not spending as much time and effort taking care of the home, being a dad, and loving Lisa. It was such a struggle to balance everything. If he didn't work as hard as he did at his job, he would risk losing it—there had already been several layoffs at his company.

Then there was the reward side of it as well—not just the financial incentives but personally. His coworkers and supervisors really did seem to like him there and often verbalized it. Right then, Jake couldn't remember the last time Lisa said something she appreciated about him. As he continued to think about it, he realized he probably liked being at work more than he did being home.

That's not good, he thought. *But it's true. They really are very affirming at my job, and Lisa's not.* He would have to address that, one way or another.

Jake took a moment to catch his breath, rolling his head to ease the tension in his neck and massaging his hands. A little surprised at how quickly he was getting tired, Jake realized that he had spent most of his energy at work. By the end of most days, come to think of it, and at the end of each week, he was weary and spent—only to come home where the same level of performance was asked of him. He knew he often let himself off the hook with the excuse of giving all he had at the office. That was something else he would have to work at.

After a couple more rounds of chopping and then stacking firewood, Jake could feel that his emotions had calmed down quite a bit. At first he wasn't sure why—maybe it was just the physical activity of chopping wood and being able to vent. The longer he reflected on it though, the more he sensed it was because he had taken time to look at his heart. He saw that Lisa had some legitimate concerns. He saw too that he really wanted to change. The way she verbalized her frustrations were hurtful for sure, but he didn't want that to get in the way of hearing her. He realized that was what Mike was talking about when he said they must learn to hear the other person's heart and not get hung up on certain words or how they are spoken.

A memory came to mind of watching *Star Trek* as a little boy. When the starship *Enterprise* would fly through a meteorite storm, they would dodge to the right, then to the left, and up and down to avoid being hit. He likened it to his talks with Lisa. Sometimes her words would fly at him like meteorites—and he would need to duck or move quickly to one side or the other so they wouldn't hurt him, all the while staying focused on Listening to her heart. Jake smiled as he visualized the image.

As Jake cleaned up from his labors, he prayed a quick prayer, asking God to keep working on him so he could truly love Lisa when they came back together to talk through what had happened.

****

After making sure the kids were occupied (the boys with homework, and nine-year-old Lea with cleaning up her room), Lisa left to go on a walk. The air was fresh and clean after the storm last night, but she barely noticed as fumes of anger and resentment welled up inside her. It made her even madder that *she* always had to make sure the kids were all right before she left to do anything. If she hadn't been there, Jake probably would have simply left for who knows how long without even thinking to check on them.

As she walked, Lisa found herself wondering if this Pause thing would even do any good. How was she supposed to "shift the focus of her heart" when she hadn't even said anything wrong—she'd just spoken the truth! *He is irresponsible with his spending and keeping receipts. God, if you're listening, it's going to have to be you who changes my heart!*

She kept moving at a brisk pace, aware at times she was stomping with every step. "I'm so mad!" she exclaimed out loud without thinking. A little embarrassed at her outburst, she looked up and down the street to see if any of their neighbors were outside to hear her. A cat stared at her solemnly from a window, while a dog in a fenced yard across the street started to bark at her—but no one else was in sight. Still Lisa lowered her voice to mutter to herself, "Sometimes I wonder if—"

Don't go there, Lisa! The thought pierced through her mind with such intensity that Lisa jumped and spun around, thinking someone was talking to her.

Seeing no one, she stopped and finished the sentence out loud, "—if I wouldn't be better off just leaving him." There. She said it. It was an idea in the back of her mind that she'd been too afraid to put into words. It felt good to get it out—at least for a moment. And yet even as she did, she sensed something not quite right.

And then?

There it was again—like a voice. Lisa started walking again. She clenched her teeth and thought, *Then I would no longer have to deal with his childish behaviors and self-centeredness.*

And how about yours?

She did her best to ignore that one. Instead, she told herself she would no longer have to hear him complain about the house or what she did or did not do with the kids. That would be nice. She could just do things the way she wanted to do them. She walked several blocks bitterly enumerating all the ways her life would be better without Jake.

What would you say to the kids? The voice broke into her musings again.

"They'd be fine!" She winced as the words slipped out, and glanced around again. *They'd be just fine*, she thought firmly and tried to think of something else, without success. They would be fine—until they wanted to give Daddy a hug and kiss goodnight or maybe have him tell one of his bed-time stories. He was pretty good at that, she had to admit, and they loved it. Her own thoughts began to sneer at her, *Oh yes, they'd be fine, until thunderstorms come like the one last night and Lea wants to huddle beside her dad, or until Jackson wants Dad to help him practice before trying out for basketball this fall, or until Cody wants to show him the next frog he catches, or—Stop!* Lisa shook her head. Why was she thinking about all this? Jake didn't really do those things all that often. Most of the time he wasn't even home.

Then how about you? How would you be?

"I'd be fine, too!" She spoke out loud again, this time not caring if someone heard her. Why was this happening? Where was this persistent voice coming from? Trying to silence it once and for all, she mentally insisted to herself that she would be just fine and that was that. Lips tight, she turned a corner to walk down a different street. She made herself concentrate on the landscaping of the yards she passed, making a mental list of ideas she might try in their own yard.

After a little while, though, her deeper thoughts began to break in again. *I'd be fine, until I feel lonely and want him to just be with me, or until the washing machine acts up again, or until I go to bed at night and then wonder if all the doors are locked, lights turned off, and temperature turned down.* Scowling at some hapless pansies surrounding a white mailbox, Lisa admitted there were some things she appreciated about Jake. The moment she acknowledged this, even more examples flooded her mind. She appreciated when he did help around the house, even if he didn't do it all the time. She was thankful when he took care of the cars, mowed the lawn, and picked up after the dog. Minor things, she might be tempted to think, but meaningful nonetheless.

Tears began to prick her eyes. Oh, why was she so upset anyway? Lisa realized how often she overreacted to things Jake did or didn't do. She thought about how easily she allowed bitterness to grow in her heart and spill out onto her husband. Her mother, who passed away three years ago, had frequently done the same, and Lisa had always resented that about her. Now she found herself becoming like her.

"Oh, God, change me," she whispered desperately. She didn't want to live a life of anger and bitterness toward anyone, especially not toward Jake. Something shifted in her heart, and she began to pray in earnest.

Oh God—do change me, please! I don't really want to be alone. I don't want to be distant from Jake or leave him. I know I get angry so easily. He can be so frustrating at times! But I suppose I can be, too. I want to learn how to be patient, how to love him even when I don't feel it in return. I want to show my children what a good marriage looks like. I can see now how much work it'll take, but I know it will be worth it. Please help us heal our marriage, God.

She had slowed her pace and now came to a complete stop. Looking at her watch, she saw that she had been gone nearly an hour—much longer than she had anticipated. Strangely, she felt a twinge of excitement to go back home and talk with Jake. As she turned toward home, she wondered how just an hour ago, she could have allowed her mind to entertain thoughts of leaving Jake. Now she shuddered at the idea—and about what might have happened if that voice hadn't spoken into her heart. She had heard her sister talk about hearing God speak to her but she'd always kind of doubted her experience. She would have to tell her what had happened on her walk—maybe it had been God speaking to her as well!

Lisa hurried home to find Jake. As she walked up the driveway, she heard the sound of wood being chopped. Once inside, she peeked through the back window to see Jake hard at work. Grateful that he was finally tackling that long-postponed project, Lisa went upstairs to check on the kids. Cody had finished his minimal homework and was in Jackson's room, trying to cajole him into playing a video game. Lisa shooed him out so Jackson could concentrate on finishing his math homework first.

Cody obeyed—then ran to burst into Lea's room, shouting "Boo!" Lea shrieked, and Lisa hurried in to forestall any tears. She scolded Cody and made him apologize, which he did with a boyish grin. Lisa sighed and praised Lea for having cleaned up all her toys. After a few moments, she left the two of them playing alien invasion with Lea's multitude of dolls and stuffed animals.

Shaking her head in amusement, she walked back downstairs to make some coffee while she waited for Jake to come back in. She hoped that he would be there by 4:30, which was when they had agreed to come back together. A sliver of doubt tried to work its way into her heart, but she shook it off. While the coffee was brewing, she heard Jake come in the back door and walk upstairs. A few moments later, she heard their shower turn on.

After a quick, refreshing shower, Jake came downstairs, following the smell of coffee to the kitchen. "Lisa, I've been doing a lot of thinking. I'd like to tell you some of my thoughts and talk through what happened between us earlier this afternoon if you are ready to."

Lisa's heart leaped. Jake seemed so much calmer than he had before, and the fact that he was initiating this conversation made her glad. It wasn't even quite 4:30 yet! She quickly responded saying she too was eager to talk with him.

Then Jake surprised her by suggesting they go out to dinner, just the two of them, so they would be able to have some uninterrupted time together to talk.

"That sounds wonderful! I'll call your parents to see if they can watch the kids."

The Work of PLEDGE – Lisa Shares First

Less than an hour later, Jake and Lisa sat in a booth at their favorite restaurant. Sometimes it seemed all they did was dependent upon keeping track of their kids and all the various activities they had going on throughout the week. Rarely did Jake and Lisa have time to be with just each other. It was hard to even get the whole family together at one time.

Something doesn't seem right with that, Jake thought while waiting for Lisa to finish browsing her menu. He would like to take a second look at why they lived the way they did as a family. It occurred to him that he had never even thought about it before. As he reflected, it became clear that this was a glaring example of how Lisa was right. He hadn't been engaged at home enough to assess how well things were going. A stirring of some kind of emotion took place inside—he wanted to do better.

After they ordered their food and chatted for a bit about their plans for the next week, Jake took a breath and said, "I don't know about you, but it was good for me that we stopped arguing and had some time by ourselves. I saw some things about myself that I'd like to share, but first I want to follow what Mike taught us and volunteer to be in the Listening chair as we start out."

Lisa suddenly wasn't sure where to start. "What do you want me to talk about?"

Jake reflected. "Well, you said several things about me when you were angry this afternoon, like you wished I would take my responsibilities at home more seriously with you and the kids. Can you tell me more what you mean by that?"

Lisa frowned thoughtfully. "I'm not sure I want to say. I think I was just venting. I think I'm over that now."

"Maybe you are, maybe you aren't. I don't know. I know you were mad and venting, but it must have been for a reason, and I'm at a place where I want to know that reason. I really want to know why you were so mad and how you wish I would be more engaged at home."

Lisa was a bit surprised at the direction the conversation was going. She'd been thinking he'd start with their different opinions regarding their taxes. Instead he was going a lot deeper. Did he really mean what he said? Or was he just going to get mad if she did open up and tell him what she felt? She decided to take a step and test the waters. "Well—if you really want me to."

"I do," replied Jake—suddenly remembering when he spoke those words before an altar many years ago.

"Well, I kind of said it earlier today. I feel like you're so caught up with work and dedicated there, that it takes priority over us. You're gone for so long, and when you are home, it feels like you're still at work. I don't know half the time if your mind is still on your job, or you're just too tired to interact, or if you're mad and don't want to be around us."

While she spoke, Jake remembered the piece of paper and pen he had stuffed into his pocket before they left. He dug those out as she finished her last sentence. Just then, the waiter arrived with their food. After saying a quick prayer of thanks, Jake attempted to repeat what Lisa had been saying, "So, you feel like I spend more time at work than at home. Is that right?" he said, trying to follow the PLEDGE process and Echo back to see if he heard correctly.

"Sort of."

"What do you mean, 'sort of'?"

"Well, you left out some things," explained Lisa. "What I said was that I feel like you're so busy at work—so caught up and dedicated to it, that it's more important than me and the kids. You're gone forever it seems, and when you *are* home, it feels like you're still at work because I can't tell if you're still thinking about your job, you're too tired to interact, or if you're just mad and avoiding us."

Jake tried again. "Okay, so you feel like I'm so busy at work and dedicated to it that it's more important than you and the kids. You feel that I'm gone for long hours at a time, and when I *am* home, it feels like I'm not really home. You feel like either my mind is always on my job, or I'm avoiding you because I'm either too tired or I'm mad. Is that right?"

He actually got it! Lisa thought to herself. *He really heard what I was saying.* "Yes! Yes—that's exactly it!" Lisa exclaimed.

Jake felt pretty good he got it on the second try. He had jotted down a couple of notes—that was helpful. He wanted to hear more about a couple things she said, so he asked, "When you say that when I'm home, it feels like I'm still at work—can you tell me more what you mean by that?"

Lisa felt her emotions going back and forth. Her excitement was growing on one hand, yet she still found herself wrestling with suspicion on the other. Was this for real? Did he really want to know, or was he just trying to do the right thing so he could impress Mike the next time they went to see him? She wasn't quite sure, but decided to say more. "When you're home, you barely pay attention to us. You're on your phone, checking your computer, taking calls from work. When the kids want to play, you do the bare minimum it takes."

Jake felt himself starting to get angry. He didn't think he was on the phone or computer all that much. And what did she mean he just did the "bare minimum" to play with the kids? Then he remembered the starship *Enterprise* idea and decided to let those thoughts slide by for the moment and simply asked, "What do you mean when you say I do the bare minimum with the kids?"

"Well, like a couple days ago, when Cody wanted to play outside on the fort, you agreed, but then you said you could only do it for a few minutes—like you had other things you had to do that were more important. And Lea often asks me if you're mad at her. I think she sees you being impatient a lot. I see it when you're with her—and I think it's because your mind is elsewhere."

As Lisa continued to list other examples, Jake grimaced at her words. This was really hard. She threw these complaints at him, and he was just supposed to listen. No, he had to Listen "to understand her heart." *I'm trying, but it sure isn't easy,* he thought. He sighed, then remembered what he'd been thinking about earlier while chopping wood, that he felt most of his energy was spent at work—and that he probably used that as an excuse to himself when he came home. He wondered

The Journey to Hope

if that was behind the occasions she was talking about. A bit of sadness came over him and a sharp pain. He hoped that wasn't what he was like at home overall. He feared maybe he was, though—at least lately. All of a sudden he found himself much less frustrated at Lisa for saying what she did and even somewhat grateful. To whatever degree he'd been ignoring his kids, he didn't want it to continue. He loved them dearly and wanted to show it.

"Lisa," Jake broke in quietly. "I have to admit hearing all this is really hard. I don't like it—but I think I'm beginning to understand some of what you're saying. It kind of ties into what I was thinking about this afternoon when we took some time by ourselves. You're saying there are a number of things I do that make it look like or feel like you and the kids aren't that important to me. True?"

She nodded and opened her mouth to reply but stopped when the waiter came by to check on them and refill their glasses.

After he left, Jake said, "I think you're right."

Lisa looked at him in surprise. She had expected him to deny what she'd said.

"I do," said Jake. "That's actually something I think God was showing me this afternoon—the fact that I do spend most of my energy at work, and how I often use that as an excuse for not being as involved at home." Jake looked down at his plate. "That's something I really regret, and I'm sorry."

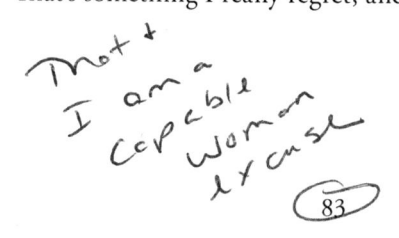

Switching Roles – Jake Shares Next

Lisa sat there speechless, and the traces of bitterness left in her heart began to melt away. It was so wonderful to hear him finally listen to her concerns and honestly ask himself if they were true. But then she remembered the things she had said to him earlier that day, and the way she said them. She cringed as she remembered how she had allowed her anger and resentment to sharpen her tongue.

"I'm sorry, too," she said suddenly, "for how I was talking to you earlier, and what I said. I shouldn't have been so hurtful."

Jake lifted his eyes to her, taken aback. *She* admitted feeling bad over how she'd spoken to him? That was a first! *Careful, Jake,* he told himself and pushed away the tendril of spite. Lisa's apology reminded him of the other realization he'd had that morning, how everyone at work seemed to enjoy and appreciate him—and told him so. How that made his job a place he wanted to be—unlike how he felt at home.

Jake decided to take a risk and share this with her, too. He was worried how she would react and braced himself for an onslaught of heated words. Instead, he saw her eyes fill with tears. Feeling guilty, he opened his mouth to say something to soften the blow or take back some of his words or—

Lisa spoke with a wavering voice, "What do you mean? I mean, what makes you think you're not wanted at home?"

"Well," he hesitated, "I often feel like—when you talk—like you don't like me, or you might even hate me. You start yelling at me, with this tone that—that just despises me. It makes me want to walk away."

Lisa's heart felt torn. Not so much because of what Jake just said, but because she knew there was truth to it. It was the same bitterness that used to come out in her mother's voice towards her father. Lisa was doing the same to Jake. She did not want to be that kind of woman! She hated that about herself. She wanted to run and hide and cry—all at once.

Instead, she managed to do for Jake what he had done for her. She Echoed back what she had heard him say. She even asked him to clarify more of how he felt when she talked to him in the way he described.

"If I had to sum it up in one word—it would be disrespect. You talk to me in a way that makes me feel like you don't respect me. As I said before, everyone at work appreciates what I do. They tell me that. They talk to me in a way that makes me feel like I matter, like I'm important, like I have value in their eyes. Lisa, I *think* I matter to you, but sometimes I start to doubt that—and I think that's when I just retreat and get busy with things from work, putting in extra hours and thinking about work even while I'm at home."

If her heart felt torn just a moment ago, now it was broken in pieces. Lisa grieved over what she was hearing. She didn't realize how she'd been driving her husband away when all along she'd been longing for just the opposite.

When Lisa felt a little more in control of her emotions, she took a breath and said, "So the reason you feel more appreciated at work is because they're supportive of you and tell you how they appreciate and respect you, but when you're home you feel like I don't respect you." Lisa's voice dropped to a hoarse whisper, "And that's why you retreat into your work."

Jake reached out hesitantly to entwine his fingers with Lisa's. "Yeah, that's about right."

Lisa squeezed Jake's hand and gave a shaky laugh. "So basically, everything we've been trying to do to make things better have been doing just the opposite! When I've tried to get you to be more involved at home, I tend to speak angrily and disrespectfully to you, so you throw yourself more into your work to find respect there instead—"

"—And when I do that and neglect my responsibilities at home, I make it harder for you to respect me and to show me that," Jake added.

"And from there it just becomes an ugly downward spiral," Lisa concluded and then sighed. "You know, I think I started realizing some of this earlier today, too. When we Paused to spend some time on our own, I went for a walk."

She grinned a little sheepishly. "If anyone saw me, I probably looked like a child having a tantrum. I was so mad—just venting everything I was feeling in my thoughts—and sometimes even out loud! But then, I started having these strange thoughts come into my head. Sometimes they almost sounded like a voice speaking to me," She laughed a little nervously, "I even wondered if it was God talking to me."

"Maybe it was. I wonder if that's what happened to me, too."

This encouraged Lisa to continue, "As I walked and talked to myself—and to that other voice—I had to admit some things about myself that I don't like. I can react so quickly sometimes to things you say or do or don't do. I don't even know why! It's like I get so impatient. And then before long—without even realizing it—I think I get bitter inside. That's probably what you hear when you feel like I despise or even hate you.

"I know my words can sound very cruel. My mother told me that once—but to be honest, I never saw a better example from her. She was always harping on my dad, nagging him and making snide comments. I think up to this point I've told myself it's okay to say whatever I want because I'm just being honest about the way I feel. Now I see that maybe I just use that as an excuse so I can hurt you back when I feel hurt."

Jake was stirred. He wasn't sure he had ever heard his wife be so honest with herself and with him. Part of him wanted to seize the moment and react by saying a few well-placed words that would underscore what she just said. Instead, something held him back. Lisa was being vulnerable, and he wanted to honor that.

Lisa thought back to something Jake said that had confused her. "Jake, earlier you said that often when I speak to you, you don't feel respected by me. I would have expected you to say you don't feel loved by me. Why did you use the word 'respect'?"

Jake thought for a minute. "I think it's easier for me to believe that you still love me even when you don't act like it. On the other hand, I have a hard time believing you respect me. When you're mad, your words just tear me down—like you're trying to destroy who I am. That's when I most feel like you don't think I'm worthy of your respect."

"So, when I speak words that tear you down—you don't feel unloved but that I have no respect for you. Is that what you're saying?"

87

The Pledge of a Lifetime

"Well, I probably feel both, but mostly not respected," replied Jake. "It's like when a person has something really valuable—say a new car—if someone were to borrow it and drive it recklessly, you'd say that person has no respect for other people's belongings. Or for another example, you say that you want people to respect your privacy because that's something of great value to you. I think that's what I really long for, to know that I'm of great value to you. But it often doesn't feel like it, especially when you speak to me the way you do when you're angry."

Lisa winced. How often had he felt such a lack of respect and value from her? Probably a lot, especially over the last few years.

"So you're saying it's extremely important for you to experience me respecting you—especially in the way I talk to you. That's how you know that I value you," she thought a moment, then extrapolated with, "And that seems more important to you than feeling loved, right?"

"Yes. Well… mostly. I'm not sure it's necessarily more important but more impactful. When you say or do things that make me feel valued and affirmed, it's like it stirs something deeper in me than when you say you love me. Both are good. The one just seems to have a greater effect on me," Jake tried to explain.

"I'm not sure I totally get it," said Lisa, still trying to Echo back as best she could, "but I hear what you're saying. Both are good but you feeling respected by me impacts you more than you feeling loved by me. Is that it?"

"Yeah—you got it. Like I said, I think I know you love me, but when you tell me you appreciate me or what I do, and I feel respected—I like being around you." He smiled a bit awkwardly, "It makes me want to help out and love you in whatever way I can."

Lisa's heart melted as she saw in him the smile and the love of the young man she had fallen for so many years ago.

Their waiter stopped by their table again to drop off the bill and bring a box for Lisa's leftover food (Jake had managed to consume all of his). Jake pulled out his wallet and handed his card to the waiter. As they waited for him to return, they shared a little more with each other. When the waiter brought back their receipt, they reluctantly got up to leave.

Gratitude

The drive home was mostly silent, though in a warm, companionable way. They both realized they had much to ponder about themselves and what the other had shared that evening. It had been the most revealing conversation they'd had in a long time, maybe ever. Both had learned things about themselves that were hard to hear, but good. They also understood more of how to show they appreciated and cared for each other. That, too, was good.

As their drive home continued, Lisa suddenly remembered talking to Mike in their first counseling session about how she longed for connection with Jake. That had happened tonight, undeniably. It was wonderful. At the same time, she found herself fearful of basking in the enjoyment of the evening.

What if it never happened again? How did she know for sure Jake would continue on this journey? She knew the answer as quickly as the questions were formed. She couldn't know. The only sure thing was that if she quit doing her part, the connection would cease to exist. She determined all the more to keep learning, working at their communication, and asking God for help through it all.

The rest of the week seemed to pass quickly—with lots of activity in and around the house—but with one difference. Both Jake and Lisa found themselves enjoying each other more than they had in a long time. They finally felt like they were on the same page and moving in the same direction, though not perfectly. They still had a ways to go. When the day of their next appointment arrived, they were eager to talk with Mike about their week and what they had learned. They looked forward as well to continuing the learning process with him as he explained the final three steps of PLEDGE.

Governed by Love

Chapter 8

DOING IT RIGHT

It was a late Friday afternoon when Jake and Lisa returned to see Mike for their second appointment. Jake had left work a bit early that day, while Lisa had arranged for Jackson, Cody, and Lea to stay with their grandparents. They entered his office a bit frazzled from the long week. Neither was particularly excited about the upcoming weekend either, since it was their last chance to finish up their taxes before the due date next week.

Mike welcomed them warmly and wisely offered them some coffee or tea before they got started.

"Coffee sounds good," Jake said gratefully.

Lisa sat down and set her purse down beside her end of the couch. "I think I'll just take some hot water and a tea bag, if it's not too much trouble."

"Not at all," Mike responded. "I'd like some coffee myself. Give me just a moment." He left the office and walked down the hall to the break room.

While they waited, Lisa reached down to pick up her purse and pulled out a small notepad. After some extensive digging and muttering to herself, she finally fished out a pen as well. She looked up at Jake after sliding her purse out of the way again and found him grinning broadly at her. He had a large, yellow steno pad opened to a clean sheet and propped against his knee as he sat back comfortably, twirling a pen in his fingers. Lisa raised her eyebrows in surprise, then glanced down and saw his open briefcase by his feet. She stuck her tongue out at him, and they both chuckled.

Mike came back into the room holding three steaming cups awkwardly in his hands. Lisa jumped up to help him, taking one that had coffee in it to Jake and one for herself that had hot water. Mike set his cup down on his desk, then reached into his bulging shirt pocket to pull out a large assortment of creamers, sweeteners, and tea bags. "I forgot to ask what you guys wanted," he said sheepishly.

Lisa laughed and selected an Earl Gray teabag and a couple packets of sugar. Moments later Mike began, "How about we start with how you guys did this past week. Were you able to practice the steps of PLEDGE that we talked about last time?"

Lisa nodded, then launched into a full account off what had happened last Saturday when she and Jake had attempted to work on their taxes. After a lengthy description of their initial fight, Jake hitting the Pause button, and all that followed in terms of their time alone and their conversation over dinner, Lisa concluded wryly, "Needless to say, we didn't end up getting very far on our taxes. Now it's definitely crunch time this weekend, but I'm still glad about how things went last weekend. Our time together ended up being really special." She smiled at Jake.

"That's wonderful, Lisa!" said Mike. "Jake, do you have anything to add? What did your side of it all look like?"

Jake summed up his side of the story much more succinctly, as Lisa nodded and sipped her tea.

After hearing their report, Mike was encouraged. "You guys have done really well; I'm impressed. You saw how inevitable conflict is. Most people are prone to keep fighting rather than stop and prepare themselves to converse in a manner that's governed by love. It sounds like you both experienced how rewarding the latter is when you take time to work at it. I can't tell you what a difference this will make for the rest of your lives if you keep practicing these principles."

More on PLEDGE

Mike gestured to the nearby whiteboard, on which the six steps of PLEDGE were listed. "So, last time we went over Pause, Listen, and Echo. Today I want to go over the last three steps with you: Disarm, Give, and Engage. From the sounds of it, you guys have already begun to use these without realizing it. No doubt you'll recognize them as we continue on."

Mike smiled approvingly as both Lisa and Jake started writing down notes. "After you Listen to what someone says, and Echo back to them to be sure you heard correctly, there is a moment in time when the person who was sharing is very vulnerable. Questions loom in their mind: What'll happen next? What will the other person do with what I've shared?

Will they throw it back in my face and use it as ammunition? Will they tell me I'm wrong or that it doesn't matter? Or will they understand and appreciate what I said?"

At that, Lisa spoke up. "That's so true! I remember having those very questions racing through my mind each time I shared with Jake more of what I was feeling. He would Echo back and I would hold my breath—afraid of what he was going to do with what I said."

"So what did he do?" asked Mike.

"He did a couple things, now that I look back and think about it. He Echoed back like you taught us, but then, he asked me to explain certain things in more detail. At first I wondered why he wasn't just Echoing. Was he going to pick apart what I said and point out where I was wrong, or what? But then I thought maybe it was for a different reason. As we talked, I felt like he genuinely wanted to understand me more. Like you talked about last week, Mike—I felt he truly wanted to know my heart.

"He did a second thing as well," Lisa continued. "I'm not sure how exactly, but he showed me each time I shared that he really *did* understand—like what I said made sense and had merit. That's what made me feel like we were finally getting somewhere, that we were communicating."

"That's wonderful, Lisa. I hear you talking about two things Jake did for you," explained Mike, while also modeling the Echo step. "First he did something that's very helpful at times. He did what I call the *loop*. As he was Listening and Echoing, certain words or ideas you expressed particularly caught his attention. He obviously made some kind of mental note of them because he looped back several times asking for more information. Each time he did, he Listened further and again Echoed back what he had heard. It was as though he needed more information to clarify certain parts, so he asked questions to draw more out of you.

"There is a proverb that says: 'The purpose in a man's heart is like deep water, but a man of understanding will draw it out.'[4] There are concerns, questions, and realities deep inside each of us that we can't always see—just like you can't see into deep water. We need someone to help us. A person who understands this principle will ask probing questions to draw us out and clarify what we are saying. This is what Jake was doing for you."

"You make it sound like I was doing something really insightful or something," Jake said with some confusion. "I was just trying to find out more about where she was coming from and what she was feeling."

PLEDGE: Quick Fix or Reflection of Love?

"That may be true. Whether you knew what you were doing or not, I still want to highlight the good thing you did, Jake. Some people take PLEDGE and see it simply as a tool to use for their own advantage. They view it just as something they're *supposed* to do when conflict occurs—so they can say they tried or claim they did the right thing. I have seen others who view it as a quick fix—a technique rather than a way of love. If they simply do A, B, and C, then the rest will surely follow. That's

---

[4] Proverbs 20:5 (ESV)

not what you were doing with Lisa, Jake. My sense is you were genuinely interested in what she had to say. That's why you looped back several times to ask her for more specifics."

Mike smiled and added, "It's been my observation that when a person's heart makes the shift so that they truly seek to love well, the right steps come almost naturally. The fact that you Listened as well as you did, indicates that your heart was in a good place and you were putting Lisa first. It was a true reflection of your love."

Lisa's heart fluttered as she considered what Mike was saying. Her mind also recalled the warm feelings she had experienced on their dinner date when Jake "drew her out" as Mike had just explained. She understood more now why that was the case.

Mike took a sip of his coffee, then continued, "Now, going back to what you were talking about a few moments ago, Lisa, and the second thing Jake did for you: he did something to communicate that not only did he understand you, but he felt your perspective had merit as well. That *something* is the next step in PLEDGE."

"That would be the Disarm step," Jake said, looking up at the whiteboard and wondering just exactly how he had already done what Mike said.

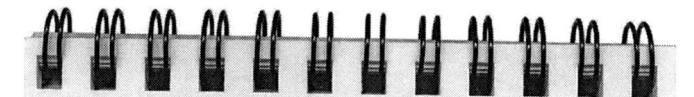

Chapter 8 Highlights

- Conflict is inevitable. The challenge is to converse in a manner that is governed by love.

- After someone shares from their heart, they experience great vulnerability. Your first response to them must be one of understanding.

- When you don't fully understand your spouse, Echo what you heard. Then loop back and ask them to explain what you didn't understand.

- Remember the message from the proverb: there are concerns, questions, and realities deep inside each of us. A person who is understanding will seek to learn more and draw these things out. Use simple phrases like, "Tell me more about . . ." or, "Can you clarify what you meant by. . ."

- Don't use PLEDGE as a quick fix or a technique to get what you want. Use it as a guide to love well.

CHAPTER 9

THE POWER OF VALIDATING

"The soothing tongue is a tree of life..."
- Proverbs 15:4 (NIV)

"That's right, Jake, the next step is called Disarm," Mike began. "As I mentioned earlier, when a person has bared their soul to another, they've made themselves quite vulnerable. The one listening can either dismiss what they heard, which will only fuel the conflict, or they can Disarm the conflict by saying something like these three magic words: 'that makes sense.' Basically, the step of Disarm is to validate what the other person has said."

Lisa started writing again. Jake glanced at her and then put a couple words down on his paper, too.

"Unfortunately," Mike went on, "when most people work through a conflict, it's more common for both parties to dismiss what the other says rather than validate them. This is one of the major reasons conflicts often don't get resolved. It's rare for each person to take the time to Listen well, Echo back, and indicate they appreciate what the other has said."

When It Doesn't Make Sense

"Okay, I have a question, though," said Jake. "You said the magic words to Disarm a conflict are 'that makes sense.' My question is: what if it doesn't make sense?"

"I get that question a lot—and it makes sense that you ask," Mike said with a slight smile.

"Here's my answer." Mike got up and stepped over to the whiteboard. He wiped it clean then quickly drew out a diagram, complete with stick figures and arrows.

Jake snorted in laughter as Mike finished his drawing. "Is that supposed to be a person or a spider blowing bubblegum?"

Mike made a face. "Okay, okay, I know I'm not the best artist in the world. This is supposed to be a car accident that happened at an intersection. A police officer," he pointed at one of the figures on the board, "approaches a young man who was a witness on this corner to get a description of what happened. Then he walks over to the opposite corner here to question an old lady who saw the accident as well. When he asked her what happened, she told him a completely different story. How could this be?" asked Mike.

"Well," replied Lisa, "probably because she saw it from a different perspective."

"Exactly," said Mike. "She was in a different location, with a different view, noticing different elements of the event. The officer had had this experience before, so he asked the first witness to come over to the opposite corner where the old lady was standing. When the young man saw the scene from her viewpoint and listened to her observations that he had not been aware of, he was able to appreciate her perspective and say to her—"

"'That makes sense!'" Jake and Lisa both finished for him.

Mike grinned. "You got it. In most every case when you think to yourself that what's being said doesn't make sense, you have to walk across the street to observe the situation from the other person's perspective. It takes time and effort to do so, but if you do, you'll be able to say 'that makes sense.' And *that* is what most effectively Disarms the conflict."

"That is so true. I don't really remember how Jake did it, but I felt like what he said and how he said it validated the points I was making," Lisa said thoughtfully.

Ways to Disarm Conflict

"He may or may not have used those specific words," Mike said. "There are several other ways to Disarm a conflict as well. Perhaps he validated your concerns by simply acknowledging he could see your side of things. I heard a speaker once teach couples to think 'not wrong, just different.'[5] What one spouse has to say on any given situation may not be the same as what the other says. It's simply a different perspective on the subject. It's not wrong, just different. Acknowledging that to each other—even saying that you can accept or appreciate their perspective—is validating."

Mike paused for a moment to make sure they were still with him. Then he continued, "From listening to your story this past week, I heard still another way you Disarmed the conflict. It sounds like you both were willing to admit not only where the other was right, but also where *you* were wrong. That's critical.

"Jake, if I remember right, you admitted seeing how you've been too focused at work and not engaged enough at home. And Lisa, you were honest with Jake about being too quick to react and speak in ways that made him feel like you didn't respect him. By owning up to your own areas of weakness and apologizing, you validated each other's concerns and Disarmed the conflict."

"You're right," said Lisa. "After I told Jake about all the times I felt like he had been missing from our home life and with the kids, he agreed with me. He said it was hard to admit, but that I was right. Then he told me he was sorry." Lisa laughed a little to cover a rise of emotion. "Simple words, but I could tell they were coming from his heart. That really meant a lot to me."

---

[5] Eggerichs, Emerson. *Love & Respect: The Love She Most Desires, the Respect He Desperately Needs*. Nashville, TN: Integrity, 2004. 190. Print.

The Power of Validating

Jake reached over and put his hand on Lisa's knee. "Lisa did the same for me. She apologized for how she'd spoken to me and admitted that her words to me can be really hurtful. She said she realized that from recalling how her mom often treated her dad. I guess I've always known my parents have a better marriage than hers did, but I never really thought about why that was the case."

"Yeah, I've really enjoyed seeing how your parents are together. I wish my parents could have gotten to that point themselves before—" Lisa cleared her throat and finished huskily, "—before Mom passed away."

Jake looked at his wife and rubbed her knee comfortingly. She sniffed and reached down to her purse to pull out some tissue. Jake spoke to Lisa saying, "I'm really sorry about how things were with your parents, but I want you to know that it meant a lot to me that you were so open with me about your feelings. Usually, when we get in one of our arguments, I just want to walk away." He smiled, "But after we had that talk, I just wanted to follow you around and be with you and help you with whatever."

Lisa laughed as she dabbed at her eyes. "And you did, just like a little puppy would keep getting under foot!"

Jake grinned unapologetically.

Mike smiled with them. "It's awesome to see how this is coming together for you both and how it's already affecting your relationship. It'll only get better as you keep practicing the PLEDGE principles and they become a part of who you are. So let's move on to the last two steps."

Chapter 9 Highlights

- The purpose of Disarming is to validate what the other person has said.
- Failing to validate what the other says is one of the major reasons conflicts don't get resolved.
- Remember the three magic words when seeking to validate and Disarm conflict: "That makes sense."
- If what your spouse is saying doesn't "make sense," you probably need to spend more time with them on their corner of the "intersection" in order to see things from their perspective.
- When thinking of the other's perspective, remember "not wrong, just different."
- Being willing to not only admit where the other is right, but where you are wrong is critical in Disarming conflict.

Chapter 10

A RARE OPPORTUNITY FOR RESPECT

"Give and it will be given unto you…"
~ Luke 6:38 (NIV)

Jake and Lisa straightened up on the couch and got their pens and notepads ready as Mike moved on to the next step. "The G in PLEDGE stands for the word Give. You both have probably seen two people, or even a group of people, all talking at once, haven't you?"

"Sure," said Lisa. "When I'm with my girlfriends, it happens all the time."

"Yeah, it's crazy! I don't see how they can hear anything! I call them the 'hen party' when they all get together," Jake teased. Lisa good-naturedly jabbed him in the side with her elbow. Jake gave an exaggerated wince, then continued in a more serious tone, "I guess it's similar in some ways to where I work, though. It's not that they talk all at once so much as they talk over each other or try to outdo what the other says. As I think about it, no one's really being heard there, either. I've often tried putting in my two cents' worth on various things and felt like it just didn't matter."

Give—Don't Take

Mike nodded. "What you're both describing is quite common. Rarely do people give each other an opportunity to speak while they listen. Usually it's the other way around. People *take* whatever opportunity they can to speak and make others listen to them. That doesn't promote what I would call healthy relationships."

"Makes sense," Jake said. "I guess that's why I don't even bother trying to talk anymore. I just keep right on working."

"Sure," said Mike. "Why talk if no one's really listening? I ask wives all the time when they tell me their husbands don't talk to them, 'How well are you listening?'"

"Ouch," said Lisa under her breath. She wondered if she had ever worked very hard at listening to Jake.

"When it comes to working through conflict and the PLEDGE process, here's how the step of Give comes in to play," Mike continued. "Jake, after you Listen to Lisa, then Echo back to her what she says, and ultimately Disarm the

A Rare Opportunity for Respect

conflict by saying 'that makes sense,' the next step is for you to be quiet. Why do you think that would be?"

"Well... keeping in mind what we just talked about, being quiet would keep me from jumping in right away and taking over the conversation."

"Absolutely," said Mike. "You either take over or you get quiet. Doing the latter keeps the conversation from becoming a volleyball game—if you remember our analogy from last session. Dialogue isn't healthy when you volley back and forth with the goal of scoring high and winning the match. Being quiet slows down the process of communication, which is especially important in a conflict. You must learn to respect the other person enough to wait until they Give you an opportunity to share your perspective rather than jumping in and taking the opportunity. You must also learn to respect each other enough to Give each other that opportunity. Then neither of you will even feel tempted to *take* the opportunity."

Jake started thinking out loud, "So after I Echo back and say, 'That makes sense,' I have to stop and be quiet. Then what?"

Two Gifts to Give

"You wait," Mike said simply. "By doing this, you're actually giving Lisa two gifts. You're giving her the enjoyment of being known and understood. Secondly, you're giving her the freedom to choose when she's ready to Listen to your perspective. For example, Lisa, when you told Jake your frustrations about him not engaging in home life, and he responded not by defending himself, but by acknowledging it was true—what did that feel like?"

"First, I was stunned. I couldn't believe what I was hearing! He'd never done that before. I kept waiting for him to say 'but ____,' or tell me where I was wrong—and he didn't. He didn't argue the point. It was so affirming. It was also a calming experience as I thought to myself, 'I'm not crazy after all.' I mean, often when Jake wasn't home I'd be fretting around the house, angry that he wasn't there, and then I'd stop myself and think, 'I'm being too hard on him.' Then two seconds later I'd be fretting again, thinking, 'No, I'm not!' I was so back and forth emotionally. I really didn't know what was right. So when he simply acknowledged there was truth to what I was saying, it was amazing. Like you said, Mike, I was able to enjoy a few moments of him knowing my heart and believing that he understood me."

"Being known and understood is something we all long for," Mike said reflectively. "Unfortunately, we don't experience it very often, but when we do, it's incredible. And that's why it's the first gift you Give to the other person by getting quiet after validating what they said. Through your silence, you demonstrate sincerity. It communicates that you really *do* understand and that what they said *does* have merit. To jump right in and give your own perspective would cause the other person to think otherwise. Does this make sense?"

"It does," Jake replied immediately. "I think of the guys at work always talking over me—it makes a guy wonder if what he said even mattered. But if they got quiet even for a moment,

A Rare Opportunity for Respect

it would show me they were at least giving some thought to what I said."

"Good example, Jake. Now here's more on the second gift of getting quiet after you validate the other person: it's the gift of freedom. When you get quiet, you Give Lisa the freedom to choose what to do next. She may share a bit more what's on her heart, in which case, Jake, your job would be once again to Listen, Echo, and Disarm. Remember the looping idea I talked about earlier. She also might quietly reflect a bit on what just took place in the conversation. *Or*, she might be ready to ask you what your perspective is. Here's the beauty of this, Jake: if you love Lisa well by Listening to her heart, Echoing back what you hear, and getting quiet after Disarming or validating what she says—she will almost naturally Give you a chance to share your perspective on the matter."

"And what if she doesn't?"

"It depends. Sometimes you'll find you don't really need to say anything else because the atmosphere between you is so improved. If there *is* something you still want to say, however, wait in silence for a few moments—maybe 15 to 30 seconds—and then *ask* her if you can share your thoughts. Think about it. You could just start talking, which might leave her questioning whether you really heard her. Or you could scold her for not having Given you the chance to share. I don't recommend either of these options, by the way," Mike added with a wink. "*Or* you could ask her if she is open to hearing your thoughts. I promise you, if you do that, she will feel so loved and respected that she will almost never turn you down. Wouldn't that be right, Lisa?"

"Yes, for sure. I can't imagine why I wouldn't unless I still had more things in my heart that I needed to share first, or if I felt like Jake wasn't being sincere. But if I've shared everything I wanted to and can tell that he truly understands and accepts what I've said, then of course I'd want to do the same for him."

"It's interesting," Mike added, "how people have the tendency to reciprocate or mirror what others do—good or bad. When someone gives you a compliment, it's natural to respond in kind. Or if you receive a birthday gift from someone, you're much more likely to do the same for them. On the other hand, when someone's harsh or critical about something, most people are quick to get angry and critical in return. You've seen yourselves how that just cycles over and over going nowhere. It can be really hard to break that cycle and even harder to replace it with a better one, but that's what PLEDGE ultimately does. And actually, that's what the final step is all about."

Chapter 10 Highlights

- Rarely do people Give each other an opportunity to speak while they Listen.
- People are far more likely to *take* the opportunity to speak rather than listen.
- If your spouse isn't talking much, ask yourself how well you are Listening.
- Getting quiet after you have Listened, Echoed, and Disarmed the conflict keeps the conversation from becoming a volleyball match. It slows down the process of communication, giving each person time to think about what is being said rather than just reacting.
- Learn to respect each other enough to wait until your spouse Gives you the opportunity to speak rather than *taking* the opportunity; learn also to respect each other enough to *Give* that opportunity.
- By getting quiet, you Give two gifts to your spouse:
  1. You Give them the enjoyment of being known and understood.
  2. You Give them the freedom to choose when they are ready to Listen to your perspective.
- If the other person does not Give you a chance to share, *ask* if you can share your thoughts.

Chapter 11

MOVING FROM CONFRONTATION TO CONVERSATION

"Follow the way of love..."
~ I Corinthians 14:1a (NIV)

"The last E in PLEDGE stands for Engage," Mike continued. "You must Engage the process over and over if you are to experience its full benefit. I mean this in two ways. First, you must Engage in the process with every conflict so that it becomes a part of who you are. In doing so, you will learn how to move out of confrontation into conversation every time. Second, each time you use PLEDGE, you must Engage the cycle over and over. In other words, you start out with one person sharing while the other Listens, Echoes, and Disarms.

Next, the one who was Listening is Given the chance to speak while the other Listens, Echoes, and Disarms. Then you switch roles once again to see if there is more to discuss. You keep doing this again and again until either the conflict is resolved or you are both at a better place relationally to make a decision on the matter."

Lisa raised an eyebrow, "Lather, rinse, and repeat, huh?"

Jake rolled his eyes, and Mike chuckled in return, saying, "That's about the gist of it, actually. Humans are creatures of habit. Once a behavior gets ingrained in us, it takes very little effort to continue—but a lot of effort to change. That's why it will take a lot of effort in the beginning: both to change your current habits of communication and to intentionally employ the process of PLEDGE in your relationship. Once you do, it will get easier and even second-nature to continue reaping the benefits from PLEDGE."

Can It Really Work?

After a moment of silence, Lisa shook her head. "Mike, this all sounds so good—but I'm afraid it's too good to be true. It can't really happen like this, can it?"

Mike took off his glasses and began twirling them in his hand. "It depends," he said.

"On?"

"On several things. Do you believe the principles I've taught you are good and helpful?"

"Yes," they both agreed.

"Then you'll need to tell yourselves that again and again, because it won't be easy—as you already experienced this past week. The mechanics of PLEDGE aren't hard to understand. In fact, as we finish up here tonight, I'll give you a handout that describes the process from start to finish."

Mike grew quiet as he thought for a moment. "What do you guys want to see happen in your marriage? How good, how rich, how fulfilling do you want it to be?"

Jake and Lisa looked at each other and back again at Mike.

"Good," said Lisa with emotion in her voice.

"*Really* good," said Jake as he turned toward Lisa and grabbed her hand.

"Then it can happen," said Mike. "Like I said, however, it will take a lot of time and effort. But it can happen. Keep in mind that if you invest heavily up front to fully learn the steps, it will make the process easier in the long run. Make sense?"

They nodded.

Do Not *Try* PLEDGE

"There are a few other things to keep in mind. First—I don't want you to try PLEDGE," Mike warned.

Both Jake and Lisa looked confused.

"I don't want you to *try* PLEDGE," Mike repeated. "I want you to *commit* to it and work at it until you see the positive results and it becomes a part of who you are."

Jake and Lisa relaxed and nodded in understanding while Mike continued. "I'm personally doing everything I can to remove the word 'try' from my vocabulary. You see, we all get excited when we see or hear about something new. We go out and buy it. We join it. We subscribe to it. And we 'try' it. You know what happens next. It doesn't work the way you hoped. It's not as easy as you thought. The results don't come as quickly as you expected. Then what? You think to yourself, 'Well, that didn't work,' and you quit or throw it away. I have no doubt you'll be tempted to do the same thing with PLEDGE. The truth is PLEDGE works if you work at it. PLEDGE is made up of timeless principles that have been proven over and over to be necessary for good communication. The catch is that you both must seriously commit to doing the work without giving up. Do you understand?"

Jake and Lisa remained silent, absorbing Mike's words. After a few moments, Jake took a breath and looked at Mike then at Lisa, "I do." He smiled slightly, but the light of determination was in his face as he spoke the familiar words of commitment.

His words kindled an answering smile from Lisa. "I do, too." She glanced quickly at Mike out of the corner of her eyes, and then back at Jake. A sense of warmth and security came over her that she had not felt in a long time.

Practice, Practice, Practice

After a few moments of quiet, Mike urged them on, saying, "Now that you've both committed to PLEDGE, I want you to practice it step-by-step in the exact order I've taught you every time you have any kind of conflict. If one of you gets irritated over something minor, use PLEDGE. If you get into a large argument, use PLEDGE. Do it over and over until you eat, drink, and sleep PLEDGE!" Mike cocked his head a bit. "Okay—maybe not quite like that, but you get the picture. You've got to practice this over and over, and just like I presented it, or it won't work. Okay?"

Jake and Lisa nodded obediently and looked at each other with some amusement.

Mike lifted his hands, "Okay—I'll get off my soapbox—except for one more reminder: practice using the PLEDGE process to help you take turns whenever you dialogue—not just in conflicts. Picture this: one person shares while the other Listens, Echoes, and Disarms or validates. Then you switch roles and go through the same process. Remember this is the idea of training. You want to be prepared for the time when conflict is suddenly upon you."

Mike looked at his watch; their time was almost over. "Any final thoughts or questions before we finish?"

"No, I don't think so," said Lisa, looking at Jake, who agreed with a shake of his head.

Mike got up and walked over to his desk to open a drawer. He pulled out a folder and handed it to Jake. "Here's some notes and suggestions for you guys to have on hand as you start this process. There's an outline of PLEDGE in there, too, with explanations of each step." He glanced down at Jake's rather sparse notes and grinned, "Just in case you need a reminder of any of the things we talked about."

Jake caught his drift and laughed agreeably. "Thanks, Mike. I'm sure that'll be helpful."

While Jake and Lisa began to gather their things, Mike got out his appointment book. After a brief discussion, the couple agreed to come in again after about a month for a progress check.

Mike watched as Jake and Lisa walked out to their car to head home. As they left, he said a quick prayer for them in his heart, asking God to help them as they worked to instill the principles of PLEDGE in their relationship.

When Jake and Lisa got home, they opened up the folder Mike had given them and found the following note:

Dear Jake and Lisa,

It is a great delight working with the two of you. The desire to learn and the willingness to look at your own hearts will be key to continuing the progress you have already made. I look forward to our check-up in one month to hear how things have gone. Here are just a few points to keep in mind for this month.

Don't look at the PLEDGE process as a simple list of do's and don'ts where you mindlessly work through the steps just to say you did it. Rather think about why each step is so necessary. What is helpful about them? How does each step govern the way in which you interact so that love is the final result?

Remember when you're working through conflict to walk through the process in the exact order I taught. If you skip a step or go out of order, it will invariably cause the conflict to once again spin out of control. For instance, if you don't Echo back what was said and just jump in with your thoughts, or if you don't wait until you are Given a chance to share, the conflict will flare up again. So even if you feel like you know the process well enough to skip or shorten a step—DON'T! Do this exactly as I've taught, and you'll be rewarded for your efforts!

See you soon,

Mike

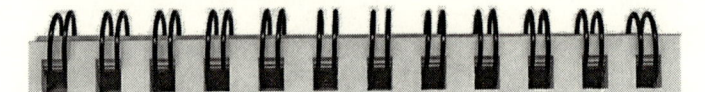

Chapter 11 Highlights

- Engage in the process of PLEDGE with every conflict so that it becomes a part of who you are.
- When using PLEDGE, Engage the complete cycle over and over until either the conflict is resolved or you both are at a better place relationally to make a decision together on the matter.
- Using PLEDGE will seem to take a lot of time and effort at first, but it will save much time in the long run.
- Don't *try* PLEDGE—commit to it and work at it until you see the positive results. PLEDGE does work if you work the PLEDGE.
- Engage step-by-step in the process of PLEDGE in the exact order it is laid out. Use it for minor frustrations; use it with large arguments.
- Practice using PLEDGE in normal, everyday dialogue. In doing so you will become so well-trained in using it, that it will become the natural way in which you interact when you find yourself in the midst of a conflict.
- Reflect upon each step of PLEDGE. What is helpful about each one? How does each step help you converse in a manner that is completely governed by love?

EPILOGUE

Jake and Lisa had many opportunities to practice the steps of PLEDGE the following month, starting with completing their taxes that weekend. With the memory of the previous weekend and Mike's teaching fresh in their minds, it went surprisingly well. Jake had contacted Matt, his accountant friend, for some advice, and Lisa worked at tracking down the missing receipts and coming up with estimates for the ones she couldn't find. They were able to file everything on time and were happy to discover they would receive a sizable tax refund.

As the weeks went by, however, their schedule quickly filled up with their children's school, homework, and other activities. Then Jake's work became even more demanding with the loss of one of their most productive employees. They had to remind each other regularly of some of Mike's words to them: "Don't try PLEDGE. Work at it!" There were days when they were tempted to throw out the process of PLEDGE altogether—or simply not address the issues at hand—such as when Jake missed family dinnertime five days in a row and Lisa allowed bitterness to grow in her heart, which spilled out in a shouting match the following week. Then there was the week when Jackson, Cody, and then Lisa got sick, and Jake was left trying to fulfill his responsibilities at work as well as taking care of everything (and everyone) at home, all while trying to keep Lea—and himself—from getting sick as well.

After a couple of especially difficult weeks with a mix of successful and unsuccessful attempts to follow the steps of PLEDGE, Jake and Lisa began to start every morning with a commitment to each other that they would work at the process until it became a part of who they were. They *would* learn to "eat, drink, and sleep" PLEDGE as Mike had directed them. By the end of the month, they were well on their way to that point.

As time went by, Jake and Lisa also grew excited about seeing positive changes in the lives of their three children. Both wondered to each other if it wasn't because of all they had learned in the way of communication. They had decided after their second session with Mike that they were going to teach their children the basic principles of PLEDGE. Each of their children caught on at different levels, but there was notably less tension and anger in the whole family as a result.

By the end of that year, Jake and Lisa were convinced that PLEDGE was changing the dynamics of not only how they handled conflict, but how they approached their relationships with each other and with their family and friends. That Christmas, Jake's brother commented wistfully on how different they seemed than at last year's family gathering. That gave Jake and Lisa an opportunity to share how God had used the principles of PLEDGE in their marriage. They encouraged him to learn PLEDGE and start using its principles with his wife and family, too.

AFTERWORD

If you have made it all the way through to the end of this book, I commend you. As Mike described in the story, good communication takes work. If there is anything more difficult than working at communication, it's probably *reading* about how to work at it. That is why I chose to write this as a narrative. I do hope you found it helpful. If I might take the liberty, I would like to give you a few more thoughts in closing.

PLEDGE is a process I developed over the course of many years and thousands of hours of counseling. It is made up of proven principles of healthy communication. If you practice the steps of PLEDGE in regular conversation when there is no conflict, you will be better prepared for when you find yourself in the midst of one.

For easy reference, I have included the PLEDGE handout referred to in the story. Use the handout along with the discussion questions in the Appendices to regularly (if not daily) practice using PLEDGE. One person answers while the other Listens, Echoes, and Disarms (validates). Then switch roles to Give each person the chance to share and practice the same steps. Remember the old saying—with a twist: "Practice makes *permanent*."

The Pledge of a Lifetime

It is worth me repeating that while PLEDGE is a process to be used as a whole in conflicts, it is made up of six individual principles of communication, each of which can be used every time you dialogue. The more you **Pause** to think of the words you use, the more likely you are to bring words of life to a conversation rather than words of death. By **Listening** to understand, you give others the sense that someone really cares. When you **Echo** back, you will bring clarity to the conversation. To **Disarm** or validate others' comments helps them know you are tracking with them and that what they say is important. When you **Give** others the chance to speak, you show them respect. **Engaging** each principle on a regular basis will train you in the art of communication and prepare you for those times when conflict suddenly arises.

Finally, if you have children or are around them, teach them these principles. You will be amazed how quickly they can learn the process. Just as Jake and Lisa saw the difference it made in their whole family, you will see the same in your family dynamics. May you experience the blessings of God as you train your children to love well!

Teach these things to your children. Talk about them when you're sitting together in your home and when you're walking together down the road. Make them the last thing you talk about before you go to bed and the first thing you talk about the next morning. That way you and your children will be blessed..."
–Deuteronomy 11:18-21

The Voice Bible Copyright © 2012. Thomas Nelson, Inc. The Voice™ translation © 2012. Ecclesia Bible Society. All rights reserved.

APPENDICES

THE MECHANICS OF PLEDGE

PAUSE and Pray (Chapter 3):

A. Someone must hit the Pause button. Usually the one who has the most wherewithal emotionally hits the button first.

B. Why can it be hard to Pause?

1. You want the last word.
2. You want to say what you are feeling at the time.
3. You want to hurt back.
4. You may be afraid the issue will never be addressed.

C. When you make the <u>choice</u> to Pause, remember:

1. It is the more loving action to take.
2. Doing so gives your emotions time to dial down and lets the rational part of your brain come online again.
3. You must agree on a time to come back to discuss the matter once again.

4. You must shift the focus of your heart to your spouse, not yourself.
5. If this shift doesn't happen, you will do more harm through hurtful words or by ignoring the issue until it flares up at a later time.
6. How long should you Pause? It varies. You could take 30 seconds, an hour, or the rest of the day. Ultimately, you must remember that before you come back to talk, the shift has to take place in your hearts.

D. The one who hits Pause usually takes the lead in the next three steps.

LISTEN (Chapter 4):

A. One person volunteers to start out in the Listening position, usually the one who hit the Pause button first.
B. You must Listen to understand your spouse's heart, to learn, and to grow—but not to defend or to build your case.
C. You draw out the other's heart to understand them. Remember Proverbs 20:5 (ESV), "The purpose in a man's heart is like deep water, but a man of understanding will draw it out."
D. When you hear hurtful words, like "always" and "never," remember the *Star Trek* illustration and let those words "fly by." Rarely does the person really mean them. They are more of a reflection of how strong their feelings are.

ECHO (Chapter 5):

A. Repeat back what your spouse has said as accurately as possible:

   1. After doing so, ask if you heard correctly.
   2. If you did not, ask them to say it again. Then Echo again.
   3. Repeat this until you are sure you know what your spouse is communicating, and your spouse is sure you know as well.

B. The essence of this step is to understand the heart of the one speaking.
C. Remember sometimes to "loop." In order to clarify words or ideas that catch your attention, simply loop back to the beginning of the PLEDGE process and say "tell me more about…" Then seek to Listen and Echo once again as they share further.

DISARM—Not Dismiss (Chapter 9):

A. Examples of Disarming responses:

   1. The magic phrase: "That makes sense."
   2. "I appreciate you saying that."
   3. "I can accept that."
   4. "I agree with that."
   5. "I apologize."

B. Avoid dismissive responses such as:

1. "Yes, but…"
2. "That's not true."

C. Never use what your spouse shares in a hurtful way.
D. If you cannot say any of the Disarming responses, most likely you have not worked hard enough yet to understand their perspective. Remember the illustration of the intersection.

GIVE (Chapter 10):

A. After your spouse has Listened to you, Echoed back what you have shared, and Disarmed you so you feel your perspective is validated, Give them the opportunity to share their perspective. This should come almost naturally.
B. If your spouse does not Give you this opportunity:

1. Thank them for sharing, but do not demand "your turn."
2. Lovingly ask if you could share your perspective. If they say "yes," then that person now sits in the seat of Listening, Echoing back, and Disarming.
3. On the rare occasion when your spouse says they are not yet ready to hear your thoughts, try to explore why and/or simply let it go. This may leave you with many thoughts and feelings inside

that are still not dealt with. Take these to God so you don't grow bitter. If you insist your spouse Listens to you, the conflict will likely flare up all over again.

ENGAGE (Chapter 11):

A. Engage this cycle again and again until the conflict is resolved or until you both are at a better place relationally to make a decision on the matter.
B. Resolve one problem at a time. If it is a complex issue, work through it in smaller pieces. In other words, share one aspect of your concern while your spouse Listens, Echoes, and Disarms and then Give them a chance to share their thoughts on it. Then take the next part of the issue and do the same. Continue in this way until all aspects of the conflict have been talked about.
C. Engage the cycle of PLEDGE for every conflict and even every conversation. PLEDGE works only if you work at it.
D. Do each step consistently and in order for 30 days for it to come naturally.

QUESTIONS & ANSWERS ABOUT USING THE PLEDGE PROCESS

Why isn't PLEDGE "working" for us?

Your hearts may not have been prepared. If you did not accomplish that shift in focus during the Pause and pray step—or if you didn't take that step to begin with—your heart will not be in the right place to have a successful conversation with your spouse. It is absolutely essential that when you dialogue about a problem, you listen to the other to understand their heart. This will only be done well if your focus while listening is on the other person rather than on planning what you will say next.

You may have had the wrong goal. The most natural goal for most of us when we talk through a problem is to "fix" the issue. But this is the wrong goal! Depending upon a variety of factors, fixing the issue may or may not happen the way you want or as quickly as you would like. *The real goal above all else is for you to take it upon yourself to communicate in a way that is in line with love.* This is the ultimate goal of learning PLEDGE. By all means, a desirable byproduct is that you will resolve much of your conflict with each other. If you love each other well in the process, more often than not, this will happen. However, whether or not the conflict is resolved, if you follow the steps of PLEDGE—*for the purpose of demonstrating love to the other*—then PLEDGE will always work.

You may have not gone through the steps of PLEDGE in the *exact order* as presented. Think of the steps of PLEDGE as a way in which you organize conversation. Someone speaks, and someone listens—but then what? PLEDGE details an organized path in which we experience healthy conversation and is the *best* plan for handling conflict. It is really quite simple when you think of it:

- Someone speaks, therefore someone must be listening—otherwise, you are only babbling at each other, not having a conversation!
- While listening, you must truly understand the heart of what the speaker is saying if you are to respond well.
- To be sure you understand correctly, you must check by echoing back to the speaker what you heard.
- Once it is clear that you understand them correctly, it is crucial that you indicate in some way that what the other person said has validity.
- And finally, out of reciprocity, the one speaking now gives the one listening a chance to share *their* perspective.
- And the conversation path starts over!

If any of these steps are skipped, a disconnect takes place, and a breakdown in the conversation will follow. It is similar to skipping a step in a detailed set of instructions, which causes the whole project to fall apart.

- If you don't Pause, you will likely argue, not converse.
- If someone isn't Listening, it is only as I said above, babbling.
- If the one listening doesn't Echo back—vitally important data to the conversation could well be missed.
- If there isn't some form of Validation of the speaker, they will experience a marked uncertainty, unsure if the other gives any credence to their perspective.
- If both parties are not Given a chance to speak, there will be obvious feelings of disparity and frustration.
- And if both parties are not willing to Engage in this or a similar process, it will likely lead to a breakdown in the relationship.

What should we do when our tension rises so quickly we can't use PLEDGE?

This is all the more a sign of how much you need to Pause! Brain scans have shown that when we are supercharged emotionally, the rational portion of our brain shuts down. Quite literally, we can't think straight!

It is also a good indicator that either one or both of you may not be spending enough time preparing your heart to hear and understand the heart of the other. You must be able to set your own emotions aside until you are given a chance to share. Doing this requires humility and the willingness to let the other person share first. Work hard to hear the story from their perspective. What parts have you missed? In what areas can you see that you might have been wrong?

Sometimes people fail to recognize that they may need to hit the Pause button multiple times during a heated discussion. When there is much to discuss and emotions are strong, couples have to go at a slower rate to work through problem areas. These problems didn't appear overnight. It is likely they will not disappear that quickly either. Talk about the problem in bite-sized chunks, working through one piece at a time. If your emotions are still under control and your hearts are still in the right place towards each other, then take another "bite" to discuss. Take whatever time is needed to be sure you only converse while your emotions are under control and the shift in your hearts is still in place. In so doing, you will keep from hurting each other further, and you will have the greatest potential to understand each other well.

While your discussion is on hold, there are several simple ways to get a handle on your emotions and help shift your heart's focus to your spouse:

- Do some form of physical activity or exercise.
- Get some rest.
- Journal.
- Pray. Getting alone with God and letting Him work on our hearts helps us dial down our emotions and think more clearly.
- You must get to the place where you are willing to hear and accept the validity of another's viewpoint.

If you work at all the above and still find your conflicts quickly escalating, then it is time to find another person who will sit with you while you seek to resolve the difficulties. This must be a *mutually* trusted person, such as a friend, another couple, your small group leader, a pastor, or a counselor. Teach them the steps of PLEDGE—perhaps even through reading this book—then ask them to coach you through the process, making sure you follow each of the steps.

Finally, when couples struggle with quickly escalating, it is often a strong indicator that there is some significant personal work that needs to be done in one or both of their personal lives. In other words, they are most likely reacting to not just the present circumstances, but to past life experiences as well.

When is the best time to use PLEDGE?

ALL THE TIME! Practice these steps in every conversation. Remember, PLEDGE is a complete process in and of itself, yet each individual step can also stand alone as a principle of healthy, loving communication.

Use PLEDGE every time you have a conflict, and use it when at least one person, if not both, have experienced a shift in their heart.

Regarding the time of day, some like to quote Ephesians 4:26, "...do not let the sun go down on your anger" (NASB). But what about Psalm 4:4? This verse says, "Don't sin by letting anger gain control over you. Think about it overnight and remain silent" (NLT).

Think of these verses as proverbs—they are general guidelines but not always the rule. The most important issue is that you both come to a place where your anger does not have "control over you," but instead you can communicate in love.

If after working through the steps of PLEDGE there is still a disagreement regarding a decision needing to be made, what do we do?

Ask each other if either thinks the other person missed a step in PLEDGE. Oftentimes, one step is left out or not done very well. You might also let the subject rest for a time while you both continue to pray. In the meantime, find ways to compromise.

Ultimately, someone has to make the final decision. If the wife wants her husband to be the leader in the relationship, then at least 51% of the time, she will have to let her husband decide; otherwise, she ends up being the one who takes the lead in the relationship. Husbands must keep in mind, however, that leading well is doing *not* what is best for themselves but what is best for their marriage and home.

Doesn't the PLEDGE process take a lot of time?

It will likely take more time when you first start working with PLEDGE. This is partly because you are still learning the steps and partly because you may have a lot of issues to discuss if you have not been able to resolve them well in the past. Once you work through the backlog of unresolved issues—and learn how to do it well—the PLEDGE process will go much more quickly.

When you think it is taking too much time, ask yourself this: how much time is wasted on unresolved conflicts or in disputes that go on and on for hours or several days?

Lastly, keep in mind that marriage is an investment. Why would we think we can get sloppy or careless in our marriage and expect it to still be good? Nothing else in life works that way. Common advice from investment counselors can be applied to marriage as well:

- Your return is dependent upon your investment.
- Keep investing every day—like dollar-cost averaging.
- Stay the course.
- You've got to be in the game in order to win!

DISCUSSION QUESTIONS

Remember that PLEDGE is made up of six separate principles of healthy communication. In conflicts, all six must be used in the order presented. It is essential, however, that you practice working with each of the principles individually or together in *everyday, normal conversation*. You will then be better prepared to use all six principles when a conflict occurs.

Set aside a time each week, perhaps 15-30 minutes, where you will practice with one of the following discussion questions. One person should answer the question while the other Listens, Echoes, and Disarms (validates) Then switch roles in order to Give each person the chance to share and practice the same steps.

Everyday Questions:

1. Tell me about your day.
2. What was the highlight of the day?
3. What was the lowlight of your day?
4. What are you looking forward to tonight?
5. What are you looking forward to this weekend?
6. What are you looking forward to on our upcoming trip or holiday or day off?

Fun Questions:

1. What would you like to do tonight or this weekend?
2. What do you like to do on your birthday? Or any other holiday?
3. If we were suddenly to go down to a four-day workweek, what would you do with the extra day?
4. What would be your dream vacation?
5. If you were given $250,000 and told before you could spend any of it on your own, you had to give $100,000 of it away, where would you give it and why?
6. You are given a special supernatural gift of being able to master any three talents you choose in one day. What would those talents be?
7. If money were no object, where would you like to go just as a couple, and what would you like to do? How about if we were to go as a family?
8. If you could go back in history and spend a day with anyone, who would that be and why?

Reflective Questions:

1. Tell me about your two or three closest friends. Who are they? What is it about them that helps bring about a good friendship?
2. Where do you think we are doing well with PLEDGE and what do you think we (or I, or you) need to work on most?

3. What has been one of the most enjoyable times we have had as a couple?
4. What one or two things would you like to see us accomplish this year in our lives together? Or our finances, or family, or house?
5. What two or three things do you find most disturbing about our country today? Or our world today?
6. What are two or three things you find most fulfilling or satisfying in your job or as a stay-at-home parent?
7. Pick three people in life that you have thought highly of or appreciated the most. Who are they and what stands out to you about them?
8. At this point in life, what are your feelings about God and His involvement in our lives?

ACKNOWLEDGEMENTS

This book has been in the making since I was a boy. For any number of reasons, including being a middle child, I grew up seeking to be a peacemaker. No one likes conflict—including me. It is an uncomfortable experience at best, and a very frightening experience at worst. I didn't like conflict for another reason—people get hurt. I have spent the better part of my life seeking to help people learn how to relate to one another in loving, not hurtful, ways. This book is a tribute to that endeavor, and I wish to thank a number of people who have helped in one way or another on this project.

First, I want to share my deep gratitude for those who were foundational in showing me what it means to love well. While I am blessed to have had a number of people in my life who were loving and kind, there are several who stand out in a very significant way:

> My parents, who have been married now for over 58 years. The security of their unconditional love for each other and for us as children was foundational in who I am today. It occurred to me recently that never

even for a second do I remember worrying if my parents would divorce. Whatever ups and downs we had as a family, we would make it through—there was no other option. Thank you, Mom and Dad, for all you instilled in us!

My wife's parents, who have loved and accepted me as if I were one of their own. I am twice blessed! Thank you, too, Mom and Dad!

Dr.'s Larry Crabb and Dan Allender. I was privileged to spend two years of my life under their tutelage while I earned a Master's degree in Biblical Counseling. I could never express enough how the training and mentoring I received from them changed my life. Their love for us as their students—and their understanding of the power of words and the complexities of the heart—is unparalleled. Thank you to you both!

Dr. Emerson Eggerichs—for his book *Love and Respect*—and Ken and Dee Canfield, alongside whom I had the opportunity to help with the Love and Respect Marriage Intensives: I thank each of you! Dr. Eggerichs's powerful affirmation of the Apostle Paul's emphasis on love and respect in marriage has shaped my understanding of marriage and conflict resolution in many ways, some of which I illustrated through the story of Jake and Lisa.

Brennan Manning. Many years ago, I had the privilege to be one of six men on a silent retreat with Brennan. During that time, I had a very unique experience where I felt the love of Jesus through Brennan in a way that I will never forget. He is now fully experiencing the love of Abba, of whom he spoke and wrote so endearingly all his life. Thank you, Brennan!

My children, you have been such an incredible support during my writing, encouraging me to keep on and that what I had to say was needed and helpful. A huge thanks to you all! When I look at each one of you, I truly marvel at the way you relate to people. You have learned well how to love others, which is a joy. You are such a blessing!

And Micah, a special thanks to you for writing the Foreword. I am truly honored. These days I watch your life more from afar (Miami is a bit of a ways from Kansas), but every day I think of you with that same reciprocity you wrote of. I learn from you every time I am around you and always look forward to our exchanges. I love the way you love your sisters, your mom, me, and others!

My wife, Zerrin, who has been my closest friend for over 30 years. Your love for me keeps me in awe. You are gracious, kind, forgiving, and understanding. You bless and encourage me, help and respect me. When I ponder what it means to experience unconditional love, I think of you! Thank you, honey! Thank you with all of my heart!

Secondly, I want to say thanks to all those who had a very real part in helping me to finish this project:

My niece Christy Wold—an awesome up-and-coming author and editor—for adding so much color to my "black and white" original draft. Your work and help were immeasurable!

My nephew Steven Wold—a full-time graphic artist—who is regularly helping me with all of our design work. You are equally as gifted as your sister—you obviously came from the same bloodline. Your patience and work with me are so appreciated!

My sister-in-law Kathryn Slade, one of the first people to read my draft, gave me valuable feedback and spurred me on. I really needed it that day!

Thank you to all who contributed financially to us over this past year—you believed in me, and that is an incredible gift!

I am grateful, too, for each of you who reviewed this book and wrote encouraging words that others might be inspired to read it as well. Thank you for giving of your time.

Thirdly, I want to say a huge thank you to all my clients who have given me the privilege of listening to the intricate details of their lives and marriages. You were humble and courageous enough to seek help and offered me the opportunity to speak into your lives even while I, though perhaps unbeknownst to you, continued to learn more in the process.

And lastly—but most of all—thank you, Jesus, for demonstrating to us all the real meaning of *love*. You chose to leave your home and take up residence in ours so that we might know you and learn of your desire to know us. When we turned against you because of our own self-interest, you loved us anyway and extended forgiveness at the cost of your life. And now you are seeking for all who will turn to you, to know you and to love as you love. I will be thanking you for all of eternity!

ABOUT THE AUTHOR

Mark Oelze has been a marriage and family counselor since 1985, helping couples process conflict in a manner that is completely governed by love. Married 33 years, he and his wife, Zerrin, teach the Madly In Love Marriage Conference. They have three grown children and live in Wichita, Kansas.

Knowing the power of words, Mark and Zerrin have a passion to see intentional love shape the way we communicate.

To contact Mark Oelze about the PLEDGE process and/or teaching a marriage conference in your church or city, you can email him (mark@madlyinlove.org) or learn more at: www.madlyinlove.org

Pause
Listen
echo
disarm = Validate what other said
give
engage